"And you?
When will you begin that
long journey into yourself?"
–Rumi

Little Shots of Wisdom That Wake You Up
to a Life of Your Own Choosing

Inspirational
Espresso

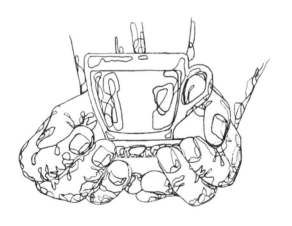

BRIAN ROSCOE

The content of this book is for general instruction only. Each person's physical, emotional, and spiritual condition is unique. The instruction in this book is not intended to replace or interrupt the reader's relationship with a physician or other professional. Please consult your doctor for matters pertaining to your specific health and diet.

Publisher: I.E. Press
To contact the author, visit www. InspirationalEspresso.org.

Artwork done by Patrick Reilly

ISBN-10: 0-9976476-0-4
ISBN-13: 978-0-9976476-0-0

Printed in the United States of America

Dedication

This book is dedicated to all the hearts
yearning to remember their love,
a love already alive within,
a love waiting only for recognition.

Acknowledgements

Beautiful projects *always* have a team of people behind the scenes that have kept it alive. *Inspirational Espresso* is no exception. The efforts of all the amazing people who graced me with their presence, skill, understanding, love, and belief in the truths of the heart are, to say the least, precious to me and have touched my own heart. I have nothing but gratitude for your help.

To all who made a difference, a heartfelt Thank You!

To Marcia Szymczyk, my faithful and most wonderful friend and assistant, you inspired and tolerated me, and then tolerated me some more. This was just as much her journey as mine.

To my friend, Gayle Gerig, who pushed me hard and got me through the first phases of editing, and we still love each other.

Lynn Hess, for your help with editing and your ability to connect with the heart of this book.

Erik Stoneburner, my technician! Thank you for all your expertise in so many areas.

Toni Houtman and Pat Reilly, for all your wonderful artistic talents.

Keith Himebaugh, for your wonderful design skills, sense of style, and exceptional connection with the project.

A huge thanks to Mary Trumpfheller and Suky Bixby for their continuous spiritual inspiration. Mary, you were so helpful in helping this book find its form.

Special thanks to Lindsey, Amanda, and Amie from Promoting Natural Health who had the brute strength to get this manuscript designed and published.

And to my great friend, Joe Sherman, with his expertise in publishing and his inspiring words, he pushed, kept me on track, made fun of me, and gave me hope, all of which was very helpful and I am extremely grateful for.

Last but not least, thank you to my phenomenal children, Lauren, John, and Ellie, whose excitement and curiosity continuously inspired me to move forward. To my father, who passed down to me his tireless search for understanding and our spiritual nature. And Mom, it was through the spirit of your unyielding belief in me that I learned love. Through you, I learned of a real love, a love that allows laughter and tears, a spontaneous, big-hearted, human love, a love worth dying for.

Table of Contents

Introduction

The work of looking within and questioning ourselves, asking who we are and how we wish to live in this world, is the work of life.

Questioning the truth and quality of our thinking impacts how we see life and helps direct what our experiences will ultimately become to us. By exploring and questioning our thinking, we create a position from which we make choices that serve our lives. From here, we can choose to change our thinking in the interest of cultivating a higher state of wellbeing and a better life experience.

Reading *Inspirational Espresso* won't give you answers to the struggles of life, but if you give it a chance and live it a little, it can help to point you in a far better direction than fear. It can help you explore things of the heart we tend to forget, and it can reopen the journey back to that spirited, ineffable part of your true nature.

As it is with life, there is no set pattern of design or approach to this book except that it attempts to help us connect with our love any way it can. It's not a *start on page one and read through to page 269 format.* It's an *open to any page, pay attention to where you're drawn, flip and pick* kind of book—so enjoy and flip on, dear journey friend!

Inspirational
Espresso

Author's Note

I am inclined, almost forced, to view my life through a lens of love:

Our purpose here, in this wildly marvelous world, is to remember how to expand into a place of deep, multilayered, unconditional love—a love that is, in essence, who we already are and have always been.

It's not always a place easy to stay present to, this place of love. We'll find the need to repeatedly remind ourselves of our truth as we walk through the trials of this world. So pay attention to what it is to be alive to the fire in this miracle of life. Allow it to own you so that you can always remember a path home when you feel you have somehow lost your direction.

In our act of "going home," we liberate our minds from the empty promises of misguided passions and reclaim our lives, we reclaim our truth, our beautiful strength, and our ability to know the depth of our own love.

I don't profess to have perfected love (and that might very well be impossible), but there is not a day or even an hour where I have not made it a point to check on myself and my path. I spend many quiet, meditative moments with myself, mentally checking-in, questioning the quality of my thinking to be sure, to the best of my ability, that I'm coming toward my world with grace, gratitude, and compassion, always trying to stay pointed into expanding back into the truth of my being. I try to bring my journey toward love into all of my interactions in this world, internally and externally. This is all I can do. Mistakes and all, it gives me peace knowing I'm doing my best, and if for some reason I don't have peace, I know my mind and heart will be searching within for the understanding and truth about why it's not there.

Finding the Truth
That Points Us Toward Our Love

Our spirited journey requires us to step back toward our truth in order to remember the essence of what we are, love. We're asked to cultivate a way of being in this world that resonates with our hearts. This is a way we already have a sense of but may not always know how to attain. Essentially, it's a journey back into ourselves, a journey toward our often forgotten truth, a truth that points us back into our hearts and toward our love. Very essentially, it points us toward ourselves.

As we walk this path with one another, we inevitably come across multiple approaches and techniques that, through the ages, mankind has developed for exactly this purpose, and we can use these to guide us. We'll naturally stumble over, get pushed toward, and even with great intention, discover some of the many teachings, understandings, exercises, and life lessons that can help us remember and reconnect to our more mindful, peaceful life. The goal of *Inspirational Espresso* is to act as a small beacon on this journey, to leave hints of truth, inspire moments of understanding, and help keep us mindfully in and living our journey, pointed toward a gentler, more compassionate way while we're immersed in this fantastic journey of living.

Author's Note

As we become more and more familiar with the

guidelines, teachings, and exercises that drive us toward spirit, they can become anything from daily prayers, rituals, and meditations to just paying attention to your breath, immersing yourself in some kind of physical activity, or in helping out anywhere or anyone in need in whatever way you can. Regardless of what you do or how you do it, these practices all have something in common: they're all tools we might choose to use to help create a deeper awareness of being alive and to reconnect with an innate sense of spirit-led peace within ourselves.

Always remember that these tools can and will be as individual and unique as each person using them. Anyone searching within to touch internal peace and his or her connection with the often forgotten "something more" knows that what works for one does not necessarily work for another. It's easy to become disenchanted with life when you attempt a mindfulness technique that seems to work well for your brother or sister but doesn't seem to connect for you, so you have to make these practices of life your own and find something that works for *your* spirit. Be patient with the journey and tolerant with your understanding.

Explore all possible ways back to yourself. Feel free to discard any practices, exercises or understandings, and if you desire, pick them up again. You may even find yourself approaching them with a freshness, seeing their value in a new way. If you have some beautiful tools in your toolbox already, great! Add new ones if you want. The more ways we explore and cultivate our capacity for more clear thought and understanding of our journey, the better our chances of maintaining ourselves in the gentleness and loving compassion we all yearn to remember. So find what works for your connection with that spirited way of being, your ability to remember the presence of love that already is, and use it! And welcome, friend. Welcome to your journey.

21

Part 1

More than a Drum-Making Exercise

In the late nineties, I would commonly get together with a group of friends at sweat lodges, and at some point, I participated in a drum-making exercise with the same group. One of these friends opened up his home as the staging ground for this endeavor, which proved to be a long, fairly grueling, and complex process. It took approximately eight to ten hours to complete, and by the time we were done, we ended up building beautiful hoop drums, about sixteen inches in diameter, each with a wonderfully complex woven and wrapped webbing on the back, holding the cowhide drum face onto the hoop. The webbing pulled everything extremely tight when the drums dried, and they had a beautiful, deep, resonating percussive vibration that lingered in the room and in your chest. Each drum was an individual work of art by the time it was complete, something worth passing down to future generations.

More than a Drum-Making Exercise

Now, I love handmade projects like this one, and I tend to be very meticulous when I'm doing and making things. I like to do them right. So I spent plenty of time with my drum, making sure all the webbing and wrapping and knotting on the back was perfectly done, and that the hide was centered on the face of the hoop so it wouldn't warp or look odd. I also took extra time planning out and executing the artwork on the inside of the drum. I ended up with a very beautiful drum. It was definitely the nicest one of the group. I knew it. I was proud of it!

As we finished up with our drums, we came into a circle with our personal works of art. We were all feeling very accomplished with our day's labor, nurturing our cut and bruised fingers, injured from pulling on the sinew webbing. As we were sitting in the circle discussing the exercise of drum-making, George, the leader of the ceremony, posed some questions to us and discussed the spiritual journey we had just been through as we created our beloved drums.

As he taught his lessons, George praised everyone for taking the time to craft their drums well and for maintaining integrity through the pain of pulling the sinew through the holes in the cowhide.

Then he turned to me and said, "Brian, would you like to learn a lesson in self-importance?"

And I, after a momentary pause, asked, "Well,

what do I have to do?"

Again, George questioned me—this time a little more strongly, "Brian! Would you like to learn a lesson in self-importance?"

This time my answer came more quickly and definitively, "Absolutely!"

George handed me a pair of sharp scissors and said, "Cut up your drum, Brian. Brian, cut up your drum."

The sound of him saying that struck me in a dizzying, surreal way. It still echoes in my head. It resonates with me any time I hold too much self-importance with anything, even now. So I took the scissors in a very aware way, and started cutting. I could hear George in the background, firmly commanding me to, "Cut up the drum, Brian, cut the drum." The webbing on the back of the drum started to pop. I could feel every strand, seemingly hundreds, sever and snap. As though I was the sharp edge of the scissors, I could feel the slicing of the sinuous fibers as I applied pressure to the handles, feeling it through and becoming one with the scissors themselves, as though we were experiencing the fate of the drum together.

Slowly, as the fibers tore away from their moorings, I could hear the beautiful, deep tone of the drum head progressively disappear. I felt the experience within

*More than a
Drum-Making
Exercise*

myself—in that moment, I absorbed the lesson into my cells. The lesson of having put my self-importance behind the things I do, defining myself through things outside of my heart. I was not that drum, but I had put enough self-importance behind its production and felt enough pride in the final product that it had taken me away from my truth, had left me stranded in my ego, and George saw that.

The effect of this illustration on the others in the group was just as profound as it was on me. It stayed with them in various ways, depending on the person. Some were mad at me for cutting the drum I had worked so hard on, questioning why I would so easily be persuaded to destroy my creation, and some were mad at George for asking. But for me, I put my lessons of the heart far above ego or desire to hold material things. I was grateful for the depth of the teaching, privileged to have been part of a class that went far beyond drum-making, and I felt a sense of completion in that we were all able to finish up our time together with potential gifts we never ever expected implanted in our hearts. We didn't necessarily like the process of the lesson, but the message behind the struggle spoke loudly and everyone walked away with it within them, able to draw on it and grow with it as they chose.

Ready yourself for unknown transformation. You never know what's coming.

Living a Life
of Your
Own Doing

"The two most important days in your life
are the day you are born
and the day you find out why."

-Mark Twain

Everyone gets sidetracked, diverted away from peace and into habitual anxiety and distortion. It's natural and it's human. The trick of the trade is seeing it, and viewing yourself with understanding and compassion.

Without judgment toward yourself, sit quietly and watch your thoughts. Observe the quality of your shifting thoughts and the ease with which they shift. Observing the nature of thought as it flows forward and away is like watching the clouds form and dissolve in the sky. We watch the phenomena with a certain awe and have no need to attach to their presence.

The process of allowing thought to naturally flow in and away without needing to attach to it allows our wisdom a space to emerge. Wisdom is like the cloud in the sky suddenly coming forward and finding form—it needs no help, just no interference, and then it's quite magically there to be seen.

We all need to understand that we are more than what we have come to believe we are. Despite all its wonderful achievements, society has not guided us back into our hearts, and it has not guided us back toward our peace. However, that's not its job. That's our job, and that's our journey. So approach it willingly and with gratitude—it's the only journey we have worth pursuing while we are on this earthly walk.

You don't need to become a monk, priest, pastor, rabbi, mufti, or shaman to know truth within—you already have it. Just stop participating in the internal chatter of the mind long enough to listen and remember the truth of your own being, to touch the wisdom behind the thinking.

No one ever said it was easy. In fact, remembering our truth may be the hardest part of our journey, but with great effort comes great reward.

"*Drop the idea of becoming someone because you already are a masterpiece.*

You cannot be improved.

You have only to come to it,

to know it, to realize it."

–Osho

27

Living a Life of Your Own Doing

We are challenged in this life to try not to feed the very tempting belief that we're only here to get more and do more, to find the path in life that helps us avoid getting caught in the idea that the journey is one of busying ourselves in accumulating money and things, obsessing over our desired outcomes, and getting stuck in our ideas of how we want our world to look. Our journey is often one of avoiding unintentionally defining our lives through our accomplishments and acquisitions.

We can't use these things, accomplishments, and desires as reflections of who we are. They can't define our truth, our true nature. This definition of the heart lies beyond any of these "things" of life.

How far on our journey toward love can any of these things or ways of being get us if we're not also feeding our hearts?

We make money to survive. We do what we need to do to keep our lives in line and organized, but this doesn't define our lives. We're also, perhaps primarily, here to remember our strength of heart, to expand past our beliefs, to touch and know the most tender parts of ourselves, and within this, we live our lives through an understanding bound to our deeper sense of truth.

In your cloudiest moments,
a path forward still exists.
Welcome to your journey.
Even now, as you hold your breath,
angry, frustrated, and sad, ready to explode...
Welcome to your journey.

The very nature of becoming one with this formed and physical world leaves us bewitched, smitten, almost obsessed with our physicality, temporarily forgetting our true beginning, our origin, our divinely inspired truth. This physical presence we're born into automatically sets us up for a journey that defines this life, a journey ultimately back to ourselves, becoming a lifelong remembering and re-creation of the very origin and identity we so easily forget.

We are all relentlessly exploring
our unknown better within.
It's just that some know it,
and others don't yet know that they know.

Living a Life
of Your
Own Doing

"Progress is impossible without change,
and those who cannot change their minds
cannot change anything."

-George Bernard Shaw

We all want the journey back to ourselves.

Our only real obstacle is holding close our own fear.

We are here to learn how to step beyond
the fear in our experience.

We're here to love beyond our pain,
to see truth behind the lies of fear.

Our work here is to unfold
the inner workings of our own souls.

"*Do I prefer to grow up and relate
to life directly, or do I
choose to live and die in fear?"*

–Pema Chodron

As we approach our lives with new goals
of achieving higher states of wellbeing,
our thinking process will simultaneously shift
and adapt to the intentions we set for ourselves.

To be patient with your personal journey
is, at best, difficult.
To be patient with others' journeys
is essential.

It's almost ironic how we search ourselves for the words to describe this precious, ineffable experience of life, an experience which actually only requires our loving embrace…yet, in our desire to communicate what we feel in these untold depths of our hearts, we create words around it, dedicated to sharing our truth, sharing our understanding of love.

Living a Life
of Your
Own Doing

It's not so much what we do,
but the heart of who we are as we do it
that allows us to make our mark
on this world.

Our entire journey is about learning to be gentler with ourselves and others; it's a journey of finding our love. Our challenge is to remember who we are, remember our beauty within, and come to intimately know our truth—the truth that has been so preciously placed in our spiritual hands. In this lies our origin and our destiny.

Follow the energy.
The universe continuously brings energy forward
in one form or another, so pay attention!
The clues are endlessly presented,
and you never know what you may find
standing in front of you, calling your name!

"If you dare to penetrate your own silence
and risk the sharing of that solitude...then
you will truly recover the light and
the capacity to understand what is beyond words
and beyond explanations...the intimate union
in the depth of your own heart...i

-Thomas Merton

We all come here with a common aim, searching for peace and exploring all of its paths and possibilities, and this infinite quality of being alive to the journey requires our loving patience with that process.

Living a Life
of Your
Own Doing

A door is provided for exit on every occasion.

Exit away from any thought
that creates disharmony.

"There is a marvelous way in which something inside of us finds what we most need next."

-Jon Kabat-Zinn

Inspirational
Espresso

If you've ever settled into the very temporary comfort of believing that you're done with any part, or even the whole, of your journey; if you've somehow talked yourself into thinking that through all your hard work and dedication to your path you've managed to do your due diligence and you've made it to the finish line of spiritual development and enlightenment; well, take heart, because this is the journey of the infinite onion, with old layers relentlessly being peeled away, revealing new ways to see and journey through this life, so I'm trying to break this to you gently. Chances are, you're not done. We're never really completely and totally done with anything. Sometimes we like to think we are, but when you think you're finished with any challenge, it's always prudent to think again. There is always something more to be learned, a new subtly different direction to see the challenges of life from. There's always an even more loving approach to be had, new ways to forgive, there's always some new adventure to be had around the corner, another aspect of something yet to be resolved. We're never "done" with anything. We just keep clarifying and purifying who we are and how we walk through this life, repeatedly reinforcing deeper levels of truth, cleaning our spirited windows until they sparkle just a little bit more. And it's through these windows of the soul that we can peer forward and gaze at the wonder of who we are.

So! Have no fear because the universe will never let you forget that you're not done. Not yet. There's still more heart to be felt, more love to be remembered.

"Your work is to discover your world,

and then with all your heart,

give yourself to it.ì

-The Buddha

Living a Life
of Your
Own Doing

Our Beautiful Authentic Identity

"By heart, I mean that part of us that feels deeply,
that experiences connection beyond the confines of time,
space, and linear thinking, that part of us that is
moved—before thought—by beauty.

That companion that aches in the loneliness of separation
so often felt in our daily lives.

That sweetness that longs for, and understands
completely, wordless stillness and silence.

That aliveness that spontaneously responds in the
universal language we call love."

—Saki Santorelli's definition of heart,
from The Healing Practice of Mindfulness

In our quiet moments, the journey
becomes one of bringing ourselves home.

Our true nature is more spirit than solid, more unformed and slippery to grasp than textured, earthy, or explainable. Like a greased pig, you can never really get a good grip on it—the harder you try to explain it, the less likely you are to hold on to it. The people who are listening to you try to explain it, but, well, if they didn't already think you were crazy before, they will be highly suspicious by the time you are done. So do yourself justice by just observing it, feeling it. Our true nature finds its full definition without the use of nouns and verbs. It exists quite silently within us.

We have a core presence of love. That's what we begin with, probably before we are, and then we experience the world, and at some inspired point, we recognize that our experience in the world is not who we are. We see that the journey is one of bringing ourselves back to our core presence. Recognizing this in ourselves and in others is crucial in learning forgiveness and remembering our truth, remembering our core.

Peace and truth will always inspire us toward our
authentic personal power—that's a one-way street,
it can never pull us away from it.

We spend our time buying into the romantic ideas that support the way we "think" our lives should be, yet what we really need can't be bought through our beliefs—it only comes through knowing our truth, knowing our hearts. It's a hard lesson to learn, probably the hardest, but nonetheless, it is the one lesson that, in the end, is unavoidable.

The simple truth is that, at your core, your identity is based directly from love, compassion, and forgiveness for yourself and all those who surround you. This is what we are, the infinitely ancient truth of our existence. To deny this, we deny who we are, our heart and our soul; we deny the nourishment that keeps us real, that keeps us fully alive. Fear creates fear. Love generates more love. This is your choice every moment. It's that simple.

Becoming more really means doing your very best to become love, to work love into your very existence—including the love for yourself when you mess up and the understanding and love for others when they falter. What better way to spend your time here than immersed in the great experiment of loving one another?

Our Job Description:

To participate willingly in the continuous questioning of what's behind your behaviors, actions, and thinking.

Question your motive, integrity, and direction.

Question what you're doing and how you're being.

This is all done in the privacy of your own mind without self-judgment while maintaining a sense of compassion, understanding, and truth toward yourself and all others.

This job has only one requirement for the applicant: Choosing to do it— choosing to learn to love better.

Over and over again we side-step the fear that asks us for our lives. Because we're stuck in our fear, we are lost, and in acknowledging and understanding that fear, we find ourselves again. In this act of self-compassion, we willingly lean into our authenticity, and remember our hearts.

"*Your time is limited, so don't waste it living someone else's life.*

Don't be trapped by dogma, which is living with the results of other people's thinking.

Don't let the noise of others' opinions drown out your own inner voice.

And most important, have the courage to follow your heart and intuition.

They somehow already know what you truly want to become.

Everything else is secondary."

–Steve Jobs

In our vulnerability, we find a strength within—we come to know our own truth, to feel our pain, our love, and what it is to be taken by life. First, we come to know it by acknowledging and admitting to ourselves that we do indeed feel, and then by understanding that this is the most integral part of our being fully human.

Take a breath.

Allow yourself to settle into that gentler place within,
that venue where you give yourself the freedom
to see a bit of your own beauty.

Journey forward, reconstitute love.

See and understand the you that is so brilliant.

Moment by moment, we always have another chance to choose to live more fully in our lives, to be more present to our experiences and to more completely embrace our journey. And through this choice, we naturally realign with a truer, clearer self-definition. We remember the essence of our identity, our authentic identity, formed in truth and held sacred in the heart. In this choice of life, we participate in our world as a spirited being with human form moving forward on a journey of remembering our loving nature, our spirit-fed identity.

Our "true nature" is that energy that is in all of its essence, you. It is the precious, unspoken energy you are. The you that existed before you were ever thought of, conceived, or born. It is the God soul expression within that takes up no space yet exists in all of what you are. This is the essence of truth expressed as (insert name). This essence cannot truly be described in words, but the words that can best express it are ones like: compassion, peace, purity, love essence, and everything that exists of love. Connecting with this love-heart identity, we remember ourselves. We turn our attention toward precisely who we really are.

"*My goal is to be aware of the presence or non-presence of ill will in my mind.*

The practice of loving kindness is the antidote; the practice of impartial kindness is the same as loving kindness."

-Sylvia Boorstein

I am not my emotional landscape.

I am not my blood sugar, hormones, income,
good or bad relationship.

I am on my journey. I am remembering who I am.
Oh, what a bumpy road that can be,
and yet I know...
I am Spirit. I am Peace. I am Love.

We are peace and we are love.
The shadows in our lives are simply levels of distraction
away from that truth.

Inspirational
Espresso

We do change for the better
when we align ourselves with our truth.

We're defined by the contents of our heart.

It's a matter of connecting with the reality of that truth,
knowing it, embracing it, and doing our best at living it.

We are all psycho-spiritual beings,
come to immerse ourselves in this physical world,
striving to remember our truth,
to know who we are in our deepest essence,
to be more fully connected to love in all its glory.

45

Listen for one moment to that quiet whisper within,
and take a breath into yourself.

OurOur
Beautiful
Authentic
Identity

"What lies before us and what lies behind us
are small matters compared to what lies within us.
And when we bring what is within out into the world,
miracles happen."

-Henry David Thoreau

Be faithful to what you are, wherever that leads...

It's hard not to watch the outside world
with a sense of dumbstruck amazement.
Don't take this magic show so seriously!
Remember, the real magic is within.

Inspirational
Espresso

Our Evolving Strength,
Our Evolving Peace

*"When you wake up to the divine consciousness
within you and your divine identity, you wake up
simultaneously to the divine consciousness
appearing as all other beings.*

*And this is not poetry and this is not a feeling,
this is a direct experience of the divine light living
in and as all other beings.*

*And until this realization is firm in you, you do not
know who or where you are.*

Our
Evolving
Strength,
Our
Evolving
Peace

*You do not know that you are God in disguise,
and you do not know that you have been born into
a totally sacred, totally holy creation in which
all sentient beings from the smallest flea to the largest
whale are nothing less than God herself.*

*And this has to be the core realization for a future
humanity, because only from a realization of the divine
identity of all things can grow the kind of humanity,
the kind of tenderness, the kind of wonder, the kind of
awe and the kind of respect that are necessary for human*

beings to live in peace with each other, for human beings
to live in balance with her environment,
and for human beings really to work with divine forces
of love and knowledge to re-create the world

in the image of God."

-Andrew Harvey

Connecting with one's heart can happen in a moment—one small, inspired moment. Suddenly, we remember something within that says: I can love. It's a vulnerable thing, easily forgotten in the business of living. We find ourselves needing reminders, again and again, as we realize who we are, remembering that we indeed are love.

Inspirational
Espresso

Even if we've spent the majority of our lives hating, or have spent every breathing hour in turmoil and painful misery, when we remember that we are not our pain, that the core of who we are is love, it offers us a gift to see all that difficulty with different eyes, stronger and gentler eyes. We can see life through the vision that flows through our heart, and again, we become a being that knows something of love, something of our truth.

Work your issues. They are calling, sometimes scream-
ing, for attention. Honor them, pay attention when
they speak, desire only to help them become something more. And when you feel tired of them, it's okay
to tell them to hurry up!

It's not what a job, school, your chores, parenting, being a friend or partner brings to you that matters as
much as the life that you bring to that part of your
world. Remembering this helps us to keep from getting caught up in expectations and disappointments
about what we think life owes us. It sets us up to approach our world in a way that creates space for us to
do well, and for those around us to feel good.

Our
Evolving
Strength,
Our
Evolving
Peace

We may dedicate huge amounts of effort to learning
new philosophies, meditations, prayers—all sorts of
self-improvement techniques and spiritual lessons.
We touch understandings and exercises that really
appear to be good things to learn about, potentially
good for the soul. But until we decide to act on, own,
and incorporate any of these lessons into who we are,
they can end up just sitting there and percolating in

circles inside of us that go nowhere. We either put our learning to the side as an intellectual achievement or embrace it as a tool for connecting to our truth. And if we do embrace it, it may actually become a stone for the next step in our personal evolution.

"We need to teach the next generation of children from day one that they are responsible for their lives.

Mankind's greatest gift, also its greatest curse, is that we have free choice.

We can make our choices built from love or from fear."

-Elisabeth Kubler-Ross

The recognition of your frailties, your fears, distortions, distractions, mistakes, judgments, and all of your glitches, delivers with it the gift of permission to change.

You can't quiet the mind and

not welcome unexpected change.

Your thinking and your consciousness

will evolve simultaneously.

Our journey here is a soulful one;

it is a gentle uncovering of our authentic truth.

"The greatest gift we can receive

is to not be scared of our own experience."

—Syd Banks

*Our
Evolving
Strength,
Our
Evolving
Peace*

You *have to strengthen what you want to be strong*
within you. This goes for both muscles and mind.

Life is not so much about developing
the things around you as it is about developing
what is inside of you.

Step-by-step we evolve toward knowing our truth.
Accept and cherish all your baby steps toward something
more. As small as they may seem, they bring light.

Knowing from the heart and the mind
are different understandings.
It's the connection of the two
that cultivates our expansion.

Over time, understanding inevitably expands for the peace dedicated mind.

Set your spear in the ground so others can dance around you and feel strong and safe.

Your dance is one of the heart.

Choose something different, then enjoy the ride.

"When you find peace within yourself, you become the kind of person who can live at peace with others."

-Peace Pilgrim

Cultivating Love

Love and fear are all-or-nothing concepts.
You are either in one or the other,
and as you exist in them,
they will color everything else you look at
with their very own special tint.

We're either looking in the direction of love
or we're stuck looking at fear.
Our awareness of this allows us
to see our choice.

Who really understands how a car works? Can most people master all aspects of all the computers and electronic gadgets, the cruise control, intermittent windshield wipers, those new radios, the air conditioning, all the technical aspects, wiring, design, and installation of everything that runs in and makes up the inside cabin of a car? Who has anything more than a superficial grasp of all this stuff? And beyond that, there are the actual mechanics—from the engine to the transmission, power steering, the braking system. Not to mention, knowing about the quality of all the different kinds of metals, rubbers, plastics, wires, and required fluids.

But think about it: you really don't need that level of understanding to be able to drive a car or truck. It took thousands of inspired people to design it, but we don't need to trouble ourselves with knowing about every molecule of its function. All you need are the fundamentals: learning road safety, a grasp of the headlights and turn indicators, knowledge of acceleration and braking—oh, and being able to steer in the direction you want to go helps. It also helps to know when to turn the windshield wipers on and off, and when the car needs some kind of fuel. The rest we can just appreciate.

The point being that all that deep technical stuff is meaningless if you don't have the basics under control, and it's the same in life—it's about the basics, learning kindness, understanding our compassion, the desire to live a life fully inspired by love and all its strength. These are the basics that get us through life in *all* its glory. We are love and we're meant to drive that car wide open, doing the very best we can to navigate any curve that comes our way, no matter how treacherous or subtle. A car burns fossil fuel, but our fuel for this journey is our capacity for love and all that love is. This is us, in life, remembering more fully our true nature.

At different times we can all get caught up in the struggles of the world. As hard as it may be to admit to ourselves, this is the world of humanity, a world of our own construction, a world where we often get stuck in our thinking and cannot see past ourselves, past our pain, or the pain we've inflicted on others. It may very well be that the most loving thing to do in this world here may be to simply approach ourselves and others with compassion and understanding while knowing that we all can always do much better, and we will all be given abundant opportunities to do so. How else can we allow the suffering and anguish we so often feel awash with to shift, except through allowing the presence of good to exist and grow through us?

Cultivating Love

Hint: If you have a behavior that is directed by or creates fear in yourself or others, it automatically limits your ability to know your truth, to be at peace, or to love anyone or anything.

You have to choose to hate. It's an expensive choice, exchanging our true nature for sludge and darkness in our hearts. This choice to hate directly impacts the quality of life and shrouds any recognition of peace.

Uncovering yourself, like loving another, can leave you feeling vulnerable and scared. It can feel almost too beautiful. However, in our vulnerability, we find strength—a strength within ourselves to be love. Within that comes the gift of letting yourself be vulnerable to another, and simultaneously learning a new, deeper way to see your soul and all souls.

No matter where we go inside ourselves, in our thoughts, in our fear or in our insecurities, we know deep within that we want to know love. Even when we slip into fear and anxiety because we're imperfect, we can understand it's all part of who we are. Trust that in all matters of fear, if we knew better from our heart, we would have no choice but to absolutely do better. This is our trusting in the best of who any one of us can be. We do this for others. We do this for ourselves. Do this with strength and compassion.

"When you do things from your soul,
you feel a river moving in you, a joy."

–Rumi

There is no real, authentic,
or rational justification for hate.

If we are love and we wish to live our lives based in love,
then hate is always temporary.

It develops as a passing emotion
if it's never allowed to fester into suffering.

We can see it, recognize it,
and know within that it only asks for healing.

When we try to deny hate or fight against it, or when we struggle to justify our hate, no matter what kind of hate it might be, we generate an energetic and emotional shroud of distortion in our minds which leaves us suspended in suffering and separated from our truth and from one another.

An emotional shroud includes, but is not limited to:

- Rationalizing our anger and aggression as necessary
- Pointing blame, unjustly punishing
- Gossip of any kind
- Existing in a world of self-important dogmas
- Any acts of vindictiveness
- Never truly wishing others well
- Anything that makes you not want to attempt love

We can find ourselves holding on quite tightly to our belief systems, our thoughts about what's right and what's wrong, what's good and bad in our world. There's a faultiness to this grasping, a tension and fear associated with holding so firmly to our beliefs that we forget our lives.

If we pay attention, we will find ourselves carrying

forward and adhering to a quality of thinking which is based in the very judgments and opinions that are all bound to change over time, bound to evolve as we evolve.

So why would we argue so hard for our opinions, or choose to hold anxiety so close? Are we not all shifting, changing, and evolving along with our ideas about how to walk in this world?

Who would we be if we didn't feel like we had to prove ourselves, protect all our very temporary thought processes? Who would we be if we didn't see our beliefs as so absolutely important that our very lives feel threatened if someone contradicts them?

Then what kind of thinking might we explore, and what quality of being might we naturally lean toward when we choose to manifest our moments in a more compassionate, understanding, and tolerant way when it comes to the great palate of beliefs and ideas that can evolve within us and everyone we touch?

Love for yourself always
translates into love for others.

Love After Love

The time will come when,
with elation you will greet yourself arriving
at your own door, in your own mirror
and each will smile at the other's welcome,
and say, sit here. Eat.

You will love again the stranger who was yourself.
Give wine. Give bread. Give back your heart
to itself, to the stranger who has loved you all your life,
whom you ignored for another, who knows you by heart.

Take down the love letters from the bookshelf,
the photographs, the desperate notes,
peel your own image from the mirror.
Sit. Feast on your life.

–Derek Walcott

Inspirational
Espresso

Love allows people the space
to be something different
than what we believe they are.

We spend so much time ruminating on what's wrong
that we forget to see and live in all that's right.

Settling Into Pain

Wrapped up in negative emotion,
putting on the fear-colored glasses,
seeing our anguish everywhere like a
conspiracy theory addict,
we settle into our pain,
by our own choice.

Cultivating
Love

Who would you be if your thinking matched your heart?
This is perhaps one of the most important questions
you can ask yourself.

Love flows forward as a result
of you being fully present in your life.

Being grateful for every moment
accomplishes the same.

When we live in the lies of our minds,
we surrender to that which causes suffering.

We vandalize personal joy,
murder our life in that moment.

Retaliate from within, live in your truth,
allow a quick death to that stubborn "self" that
yearns to feel so important.

Finally see who you are.

You are large beyond imagination,
and so worthy of all that love is.

We often mistake our anxious thoughts for our reality,

but in truth, they only point us toward anger,

emotional reaction, and fear—never toward our peace.

————

Fear obscures the soul.

————

In love,

anxiety turns into interest or concern,

and fear might become excitement.

A low state of wellbeing can always

be evaluated and traded for a higher one.

Cultivating Love

————

Love naturally constructs its own wide berth...how

fortunate for us!

Give yourself permission to love in every circumstance.
However life appears to us, this is how
we bring quiet to a world that seemingly feeds
on the chatter of fear.

Refuse to see your life with the eyes of a victim.
In doing so, you release yourself to explore the freedom
that flows through your being.

Your mistake is believing that the everyday life situations
and difficulties around you are life-threatening,
when in reality, they are just everyday life situations.
When you can see them more simply as life unfolding,
it allows you to walk toward life's situations
with less fear, more gentleness, strength,
and with more overall compassion.

Love is not a quantifiable item!
You can't calculate the amount of love that exists within.
Love simply is, or it's shrouded by fear.
There's a clear, yet sometimes hard to define,
on/off switch here.

" Love sometimes wants to do us a great favor: hold us
upside down and shake all the nonsense out."
-Hafiz

When you feel conflicted or unsure about something,
ask yourself:
What would love do now?
And listen.

"*Fear is a natural reaction to moving closer to the truth.*"

-Pema Chodron

Fear is the mother of trivial thinking and anxious children.

In choosing a life, do it with love, because the alternative is no fun for anyone.

Inspirational
Espresso

Even in our poorest moments, grace will attempt to fill the space around us.

It's up to us to stay open to that.

Where our love might take us we hardly know. Every-
thing feels worse when perceived through fear.

When I allow myself to feel unlovable,
it's impossible for me to be loving and free,
and to fully be myself.

When we're stuck in "future fear," we stunt our life
experience and we end up basing our awareness
in self-generated limitation and anxiety.

Questions to ask yourself:

Once fear is eliminated, what do you have left?

What comes after the elimination of your fear?

Who are you after fear no longer influences your choices?

"*The only real difference between anxiety*
and excitement was
my willingness to let go of fear."

−*Barbara Brown Taylor, Learning to Walk in the Dark*

Inspirational
Espresso

Living in fear always subverts the journey,
at least temporarily.

When we live in fear-based belief systems,
we feel like we have to protect ourselves from the
"enemy," whatever or whoever that might be.
Living from our truth, we see a friendlier world,
one that needs our compassion and our strength.

"There are no human enemies,
there are only people in pain
asking for help."

–Sylvia Boorstein

Surround yourself with the beautiful
that's already within you.

Everything that we are,
every aspect of who we truly are,
it's all more important than the fear we so cling to.

Fear controls with no advantage to the
body, mind, or spirit.

Not exactly a win-win scenario.

Entertaining Love

Love requires no fear, no vengeance, no hate,
and no contempt.

It's a low maintenance kind of emotion,
and we are here to learn how to love one another,
not fear one another.

Period.

Claiming Freedom

*"Everything can be taken away from a man
but one thing: the last of the human freedoms to
choose one's attitude in any given set of circumstances,
to choose one's own way."*

-Viktor Frankl, Holocaust survivor & psychiatrist

To be free of the good opinions of others does not suggest that we reject their opinions. It suggests that our desire to please others and have them think well of us can have the power to subvert our own truth, leading us to live our lives trying to impress them by showing that we agree with them or that we are enough. In our human desire to belong, we can be tempted to do this rather than be more fully alive to ourselves and be in our own truth. And regardless of all that, being free of others' good opinions of us is just an easier, stronger, and happier path to walk.

It's a relentless part of the process of being human—returning to ourselves, time and time again, remembering and reminding ourselves that we're on a journey, that this earthly walk is a path toward our essence. We are all immersed in the continuous thoughts and acts of claiming our freedom, reclaiming our love, embracing our truth, and on the natural journey into places of forgiveness. All of these concepts naturally pull together and explode within the heart, your heart, a heart that demands nothing less than truth of love.

Trapping Rabbits

When I was five years old, I trapped rabbits for a living. Though never triumphant, I was a determined hunter. I was a big Daniel Boone fan. So one afternoon, as I was returning from one of my hunting expeditions, I had a profound experience regarding the choice of love.

I'd been poking around in the woods across the street and down the hill from our house. There was a small outcrop of trees right next to a farmer's field ripe with wild grapes, great climbing trees, and many (in my mind) perspective rabbits. After a day of unsuccessful trapping, I decided to walk back toward our house, and I heard my parents in yet another one of their loud arguments. (Note: My parents were two only children. They had lots of passion, desperately loved one another, but each rejected any attempts at the other's control of them—just lots of misunderstood ego, occasional bursts of anger, and lots of lovin'. They were doing their best to find themselves, and defining their young love required some very electric arguments, which were always beyond my understanding, always upsetting to my sensitive ways, and always made it worthwhile for me to stay in the woods a bit longer.)

On this particular summer day, while walking toward our house, I heard my parents arguing all the way from across the field. It was a good one! I stopped and lingered a bit longer on the hill, hoping for things to subside a bit. I was five and I was confused. I didn't understand adult arguments and had no idea what to do with the pain I felt around my parents yelling at each other. So I looked up and talked to the sky. I asked questions: *Why do they do this? Why do they hurt each other and argue so much? Why can't they just be nice to each other?* I wondered why people just couldn't be nicer to each other, even me. I wanted to be nicer. I was quite the disheartened five-year-old.

Almost automatically, words entered my heart and my mind.

"It doesn't have to be this way, Brian. There's a better way, Brian, with more love. There's a better way and it doesn't have to be this way. There's a better way with more love."

I felt great peace and happiness having heard and felt this truth. I had a sense of reassurance that settled into me as a child that life could indeed be better. I remember thinking, *Boy, I'm pretty smart!* I didn't know where that came from, but being five, I'm pretty sure I took full credit for it.

Understanding filled me in that moment, and then my little world moved forward, as they do, into adulthood. I lived my life, had my own arguments and my own difficulties, went through the many struggles of being alive, and over and over again, tried to wake up, or maybe better put, tried not going to sleep. My truth of a better way was often acknowledged and reached for when I could recognize that I was spiraling into untethered fear and anger. My life was always begging for a greater understanding around the pain of life. Having that touchstone of love in my mind and close to my heart always helped bring me back to that more centered space within, back to a truth-based and compassionate way I already knew. Often, I only needed to learn to notice when it was not present, when it was sleeping, so I knew to wake it back up. Being mindful requires this. It asks us to be present with whatever we are dealing with in the moment, without judgment. This is how we fill the spaces that used to be filled with fear and ill will with love, understanding, wisdom, and compassion.

The questions of who we are and how we should live come back to us over and over again, and as we get closer and closer to knowing our truth, we will always answer life's questions with love.

In my five-year-old epiphany, I evoked an awareness that helped me understand and define a direction for this journey. We have the capacity to choose love, to function from a loving place, even if it seems difficult. I heard and felt this "better way with more love" from within, a gift from the sky, a lesson in listening to an eternal truth.

Knowing that you are ultimately not in control
and never were can either traumatize you
or set you free.

Perhaps ultimate control exists in the space
we were never meant to understand, or, even better,
in our ability to choose how we respond to the parts
of our world we can never control.

"Your life is the sum result of all the choices you make,
both consciously and unconsciously.

If you can control the process of choosing,
you can take control of all aspects of your life.

You can find the freedom that comes
from being in charge of yourself."

–Robert F. Bennet

Inspirational
Espresso

To more fully love one another, we need to allow others
to make their own choices without judging them—free
them from our opinions, and free ourselves from our
attachments to who we think they should be.

The more grounded we are in our love,
the more we can see and respond to our
old issues differently.
There's a lot of freedom in that.

Our only real job is to approach ourselves
and everybody else as gently as we can
in a world that doesn't always encourage that.

Claiming
Freedom

"$\mathcal{T}$he best years of your life are the ones in which you
decide your problems are your own.
You do not blame them on your mother, the ecology, or the
president. You realize that you control your own destiny."

–Albert Ellis

You choose the way you want to see life,
and that will determine how you live it.

Your choices and the quality of thinking you adopt from
within determine the tone of your experience,
define the lens you are looking at life through.

Don't make the mistake of believing that anything
but your own true nature should be given

the power to dictate those choices for you.

The way you choose to think is the way

You *choose...*

…no one and nothing does it for you.

In giving up your contrived dream about something
and how that something should be,
you free yourself from that dream.
You free yourself from dreaming in a belief system
that restricts you.

Be happy where you are and open to the idea
of being in your journey,
no matter where it leads you.

How many choices do you make through the day
that are made of chains, leaving you running
on automatic, vulnerable to fear, and
a prisoner to your old ways?

Claiming
Freedom

In fear, we give up our freedom. We end up walking around in internal turmoil and a pain we have contrived and given life to. We surrender to living in a space where we can no longer trust ourselves to know what is true.

Living freely, in the presence of and guided by love and compassion, we allow natural movement toward our authenticity, expansion of the heart, and toward others more gently. It's a win-win way of being in life, bringing peace instead of turmoil and forgiveness in all directions.

We live our self-definition. We are far more defined by the limits we place on ourselves than by any limits others place upon us.

Embracing Our Truth

"We are who we are,
even if we sometimes forget."
−Men in Black 2

How often are our responses to one another based out of "post-traumatic life syndrome?" How often are we responding in particular ways because we can't say things without first running them through that stagnating lens of past memory?

Once our awareness of the lens becomes evident to us and we see its impact on us in its deeper, more cellular way, it's impossible for us to go backward, back to mindlessly reacting with old patterned responses, living unaware of ourselves and our choices. The heart-mind won't allow it. If you try, you end up watching yourself thinking and acting ridiculously. If that's not a depressing sight, I don't know what is. Talk about motivation for change! When you understand the distorting qualities of the lens you've been using, you're automatically put in a position where you have to change, where you cannot not change.

With new knowledge remembered and fused into your heart, it's impossible to go on as you always have. You know a better way within yourself, a better way of being here in this world.

There is an endless quality to this work of remembering ourselves, and as we release our rigid thinking and preconceptions, we allow infinite new thought and understanding to flow forward, in and through us.

"*Love is not a mere sentiment.*

Love is the ultimate truth at the heart of creation."

-*Rabindranath Tagore*

There can be a faultiness behind believing that we need to do something to reclaim our sense of spirit, to remember our truth, our true nature, as though truth, love, or our compassion is too fragile and can be easily crushed and brushed away. When we forget that we are endowed with and constructed by all the abundance of the world, when we forget the infinite origin of our creation, the perfection of our spirited form, we can deceive ourselves into seeing ourselves as broken and needing to be fixed. But we're not broken. There's nothing about us that actually needs to be fixed. We do, however, need to continuously attend to and adjust the quality of our thinking. We need to uncover ourselves, embrace our light, that essence that we already are—but nothing about that needs to be fixed. We simply need to allow the uncovering of our brilliance. Another way to put it might be that it's not as much about waking up as it is about not going to sleep. We were created awake—that doesn't break, it only gets forgotten. Now this does not mean that our uncovering is easy by any means. It could be the most challenging thing we have to endure in this life. And this does not mean we are flawed. Perfection creates us perfectly; we just need to get out of the way. Therein lies our challenge. With a breath of understanding and compassion, we remember what we are so that we can express the life energy that fulfills us, and spark that spirited memory of our truth that so turns us on!

So, the core of our journey is remembering the better way. In a nutshell, it means re-learning what we already know, re-learning through the whispers of our heart how to connect to and cultivate the deep understanding and peace that naturally exists within ourselves. And if we so desire, and we *all* do, we can listen for these teachings through quiet contemplation in the silence of our being.

Be patient with yourself. Your journey is always one of the heart. It's important not to get caught up in placing any kind of judgment or values on its progress. Be peaceful in the fact that you can touch your internal understanding, choose to step forward over and over again on your sacred path of life. Be grateful for the cultivation of truth within, however it opens to you, and know that you are always on a truer, more alive, gentler path, free of anything but being fully present in your journey.

Be free of the good opinions of yourself and others'. You are not here to please anybody or to be pleased by anybody. You are here to remember yourself, which will, oddly, please everyone anyway, whether they know it or not.

Your job is to simply do your best to maintain a direction with heart. We will remember ourselves. It's impossible not to. Best to do it while you're still here.

Be the vehicle of your own happiness—after all,
you're the driver!

We continuously expand back toward ourselves as we
stare into the smoke-stained mirror, un-shrouding,
undressing into our nakedness, exposing our truth, so
that we may see our lusty, succulent selves, and smile.

Bottom line: We are designed to heal,
and often the greatest disruption of the healing
is our disbelief that it's true.

There's nothing so important in life
that it is worth forgetting yourself for.

"Fear is a natural reaction to moving
closer to the truth."
-Pema Chodron

One of the tricks of life
is recognizing unproductive anger
and letting it teach you.

Yearning: A tender or urgent longing motivated by love.

We are all those who yearn for an unknown better.

We yearn for that place within, that unknown better which exists to be explored in every heart. We are on our journey of continually moving toward it, and never fully grasping hold, always seeking more.

It is infinite strands of unknowability, after all, something that can only be felt with the heart.

Inspirational
Espresso

Inspiration simultaneously strikes the mind
and the heart.

Our personal experience of this life comes down

to this simple, very personal understanding:

I, think me.

No one else can do our thinking for us.

We choose the way we view our world.

Truth needs no fancy presentation,

just a little attitude.

It is our choices that show what we believe we are.

It is our heart, un-shrouded and free of fear,

that allows and inspires us to reveal our truth.

"*It is only possible to live happily ever after
on a moment-to-moment basis.*"

~ *Margaret Bonnano*

---

*Healing begins with the acceptance of the gift of our
life—embracing with the whole of who you are,
heart and soul, the life you have been given.
Our role is to step forward with full immersion
into all that life can be.*

*You cannot intellectualize your way to a spirited life.
You need to feel it and let it become you.*

Justice and kindness operate with similar agendas
in our journey of becoming more.

Each requires love and patience to be real.

Our connection with wisdom and compassion
will determine what this looks like,
and it's essential to be able to make healthy distinctions
in order for us to apply their appropriate use.

Your truth does not come from anything
outside your skin.

As a matter of fact, your skin is not even
an adequate boundary.

Breathe.

Your truth breathes through you like
blood runs through your veins.

It is silently felt.

Embracing
Our Truth

Love is the way we grasp and understand another
human at the core of their truth.

I Love the Courageous

Impressive are the people who are willing to look at and see themselves, willing to open up and look for the clarity that exists within.

When we choose, we all have the insight and courage to recognize and admit that we're feeling a particular way, grabbing onto a particularly difficult emotion that keeps us from stepping toward being in our life, lovingly. When we can look this disruptive feeling in the eye and understand that our anxious attachment to this emotional glitch does not have to define us, it sets us free to expand back toward our true nature. We're willing to see our life differently, exploring our truth, opening to our yet to be explored, unknown better way. Our need to continue suffering in the emotional clamor ceases, and instead, if we choose, we learn from it—allow the temporary emotional detour to teach us how to find our way back toward love.

Inspirational
Espresso

"The strongest principle of growth
lies in the human choice."
-George Eliot

*Your innate wisdom may be prompting you
to do absolutely nothing in a particular situation—and
that may be just perfect.*

---

*All thoughts that guide us toward balance
are inspired thoughts.
No matter how big or how little they seem
in the moment,
be sure they are inspired from
love's presence within.*

---

*We are here to help one another navigate
the difficult times and to embrace happiness,
no matter how it differs from our own.*

*"Something wonderful begins to happen with the
simple realization that life, like an automobile, is driven
from the inside out, not the other way around."*

-Richard Carlson

*When you feel stuck in negative thought,
know that there is always a better way,
that there's knowledge to be had through your experience,
and that your state of wellbeing just hasn't quite caught
up to your heart...yet.*

*Wisdom is always just around the corner,
waiting for you to have a peek.*

*Understand that behind this place of churning thought
is the potential for inspiration and wisdom—a wisdom
that makes the next churning moment either gentler
or unnecessary.*

*The trick is understanding what you have
control over and what you don't.*

It's the way you think about anything that's your choice.

*Wisdom is not always pleasant,
but it always feels like the cleanest choice.*

---

*Embracing
Our Truth*

Words just don't do full justice to truth.

Journey into the Forgiving Heart

"There comes a time when it is vitally important
for your spiritual health to drop your clothes,
look in the mirror, and say, 'Here I am.
This is the body-like-no-other that my life has shaped.
I live here.
This is my soul's address."
—Barbara Brown Taylor, An Altar in the World:
A Geography of Faith

Forgive them, they know not what they do...

This isn't just a forgiving little quip oriented at the crucifiers of Jesus, but a deep-set suggestion for a lifestyle change for all. People can be in complete denial or ignorant justification that they may be creating pain for others, and a shift is desperately needed by the heart.

We can get stuck in our anger at the actions of others because our egos know these "evil doers" are to be blamed for their ignorance, but thank God for our spirit, because it has already forgiven them. So ask yourself: Do you want to hold on to this with ego or with spirit?

When we haven't cultivated our ability to walk in self-forgiveness, it's impossible to forgive those around us, whether they did anything wrong or not. We can define ourselves and others by the mistakes we make or use them to clarify who we don't wish to be.

Forgiving yourself for your mistakes and your human ways can only help make the weight of this journey lighter—lighter for you and for those around you.

A good step in our journey might be to forgive this life for its complexities and difficult qualities. This opens us up to walk forward with more gratitude and to cultivate a deeper love for life.

Understand that, in life, mistakes happen.
Allow yourself the freedom of that…but
don't overindulge. It's rude!

Our quality of forgiveness toward another
can be calibrated by paying attention to the level
at which we are able to "wish them well" in our heart.
If there is any reservation at any level, then we know
that we're not done, that there's more work to do.

Surround your memories of others with goodwill
and compassion, and in your mind,
allow them to walk away as you wish them well.

Forgiveness is only from you.
It's your gift to yourself, through yourself.

Maintain slow, defined progress
around doing your best.
You'll be able to look back knowing
your path had passion.

Those around us can seem so loud, so difficult, so painful.
Our ability to see them with compassion
is the work of life.

Inspirational
Espresso

Seeing Pscyhological Innocence

Seeing ourselves and others in their psychological innocence helps us step forward in life with a quality of wellbeing that allows forgiveness to come to us. It inspires us to see others and ourselves as beings that have quite understandably made mistakes, rather than beings that are themselves mistakes.

As Maya Angelou said, "When we know better, we do better."

There is often a lingering pain that always bubbles within us when we know that we could have chosen better, that our thinking and behavior could have put peace over suffering. This is the crossroad where forgiving yourself can set you free to do better. This is the jumping off point where you can learn to fly.

Journey into the Forgiving Heart

Note to self: How about wishing yourself well?

Changing the negative energy we have toward ourselves is essential. Forgiving ourselves for what we have thought about, acted on, and done in the past, and then being able to see ourselves in psychological innocence is mandatory. This not only applies to having compassion for and forgiving ourselves, but is essential in stepping forward and doing the same for others.

Inspirational
Espresso

Understanding
Our Innocence

Each of us experiences life on our own terms, meaning that our experience is based out of the opinions, positions, beliefs, and attitudes we hold close to. Like the saying goes: "The only thing we ever really control is the attitude we bring into the room." The same can be said for the life experience. It is defined through the attitudes we hold close to and carry with us. There's no other choice—we perceive the world based on our personal understandings and judgments that we hold as real. When we can understand that this applies equally to us all, suddenly our differences all share a similarity. We recognize that each of us is seeing life the only way we can, through the unique lens of our personal knowledge, and that's what is determining the quality of how we see our experiences, whatever they may be.

We will each, in our own unique way, see life differently because we have all experienced our lives in a uniquely individual way. And as we honor and strive to understand the extent of how different our experiences, and subsequently ourselves, can be, it allows us to give one another the loving space to get to know and connect with our truths.

Bringing this loving space to one another is how we

approach seeing ourselves and others in psychological innocence. It adds a new light to the old adage, "Give them a break, they're only human!"

Psychological Innocence:
A complicated way to say,

"Give yourself and everyone else a break
before you get stuck in your judgment!

We're all doing our best,
given where we've been and what we were
exposed to or not exposed to along the way."

It is the most common of human characteristics
that our state of wellbeing be challenged
by our internal and external environment.

Whatever the situation may be, our best is all we have.

It's by forgiving ourselves and others for being human
and not being perfect that we maintain ourselves in a
state of wellbeing congruent with our hearts.

"My life is my message."

-Mahatma Gandhi

My journey doesn't seem so distant, so unattainable, when I can serve others. As I expand myself toward my own peace, I know I'm also automatically touching and influencing others in the hopes that love will spread. My wish is for a domino effect in the world, so that at some small level, domino by domino, we will all be inspired to take steps toward knocking down the many obstacles to our own peace, steps toward replacing our fear with the resonance of love's presence.

105

Journey into the Forgiving Heart

We are all put here as perfectly imperfect beings.

We all know it deep down, and yet we struggle to forgive those who stumble in their imperfections, or to forgive ourselves for our own mistakes.

But we have great ability, and we can walk with more compassion than this, because non-forgiveness is not our true nature, not our truth.

*When we forgive, we allow another their imperfections,
and in our hearts we hope for something more,
something better for them and their life.*

*In doing so, we free ourselves of all the toxic thoughts
associated with the words and acts resulting
from their mistakes.*

*We give everyone the permission and opportunity
to start fresh within themselves.*

Inspirational
Espresso

Beginning Again, Redefining Your Journey

"Whether you and I and a few others will renew the
world some day remains to be seen.
But within ourselves, we must renew it each day."

-Herman Hesse

Over and over again we're presented with the curious, sometimes painful, often unanswerable questions of life. Life bestows questions and bears precious lessons, sometimes gently whispered, but often dropped in our lap like a rattlesnake.

When we're dedicated to our journey, it's unavoidable. We're repeatedly challenged to question ourselves about the quality of life we're generating. Poised in our journey, we quietly ask ourselves what quality of thought we're bringing to our answers about anything we encounter. In questioning if we're willing to learn the lessons presented, can we approach the gift in whatever package it comes? Can we sidestep our personal opinions, challenges, and old ideas and reset ourselves into that honored place within that expresses our truth? We know how to operate outside our truth, how to get stuck in our fear, our judgment, but have we chosen to cultivate the ancient skills still lay deep within that only want to seduce us into the exploration of our love?

If your answer is *yes*, welcome to your beautiful journey. If your answer is *no*, well…in that case, welcome to your beautiful journey. The only difference will be the quality of how you experience it, the heart that exists in your choice.

So welcome to your journey, friend.

A Little Better

Learn how to appreciate when things become "a little better." A little better has a way of folding into itself and multiplying internally. A little better over time accumulates into "this is better." Celebrate your quarter step forward rather than sitting in the unrealistic expectation of trying to do everything perfectly. Perfect performance is impossible. We can never reach perfection in this environment, nor are we meant to. We are meant to continuously try to do our best over and over again with the objective of spiraling upward toward a greater understanding of our truth...*that* is our perfect.

This comes up over and over again within—me asking for release from pain. Not because my heart wants to know no pain, but because it understands that pain and suffering are different. Suffering is a pointless endeavor, fruitless in its efforts, creating no lessons, simply spiraling back into itself. We know we're in a mode of suffering when we refuse to hold the pain part of life differently, when we refuse to see it with a potential for something more—and when I'm stuck, I absolutely want out of my suffering, I want to understand with fresh vision.

Pain exists for all of us. However, our understanding about its nature is very different from suffering. Pain is eager for release and healing, willing to change, eager to be filled in with new thought. Pain exists in our lives and it's our choice to learn from that pain. Pain is happy to be temporary. Suffering wants permanence that goes nowhere. So peek behind the discomfort and find your permission to transform—a permission only we can give ourselves, over and over again.

As we move closer to our truth, we become acutely aware of how distorted our thought process can be. Our anger, our depression and despair, our irrational frustration, our self-important banter, and even how we think about love all wiggles through our minds and we become uncomfortable observers of our thoughts and our lives. Suddenly, we have to stop. We find that we can't tolerate our own ignorance any longer because what could be more unbearable than feeling away from our truth? And we start again, as often as we need to, we begin again, each time with a new freshness and a hope for something better.

When we're stuck in pain, feeling unable to see any light, it's here that we need to find a way to let ourselves know that there's often folly in the way we think. And we need to see that there's also something different to be had, an understanding far bigger than the suffering we're stuck in. We need to understand that there's choice to be had, that we can *always* think differently, and we will absolutely be able to choose something better.

———————

Redefining your journey:

You must recalculate the equation
when the answer to the question in front of you
doesn't match the answer that is already written
within you.

———————

One of the greatest stress reducers of all time
may just be our ability to pull back from our future
and past oriented thinking,
and let ourselves be fully alive
to this present moment right now.

Breathe

Take a breath and…re-center, recalibrate, reconnect,

reset, renew, and

breathe… just……..breathe.

With every breath, fresh thought is given
the opportunity to germinate.

Expanding into our journey only requires
that we keep breathing!

So by all means, keep breathing,
and stay awake to your cherished art of being.

Dance your own best dance as you show yourself
who you are, even if you don't entirely know.

Just go in the direction that your energy,
your authentic heart, pulls you.

And know that you can't fit into a world
that's not yours, a world that belongs to fear,
whether it be yours or another's.

As we cultivate our ability to step away from
our temptations of anguish and personalized conflict,
we develop our capacity to move back toward love.
That's what we are, and this journey challenges
and assists us over and over to continue
pointing ourselves in that direction.

"In the confrontation between the stream and the rock,
the stream always wins—not through strength
but by perseverance."

–H. Jackson Browne

Grouchiness is just a residual effect
of living in distorted thinking.
That cranky, bad mood of unexplained origin
came from somewhere.
Ask yourself: What have you been thinking?
And then think again.
There's always room for improvement!

Our hope is in our choices.

We can always choose again.

"*So even if the hot loneliness is there,
and for 1.6 seconds we sit with that restlessness
when yesterday we couldn't sit for even one,
that's the journey of the warrior.*"

–Pema Chodron

---

*How many ways, how many times every day,
moment after moment, can we begin again,
start again, point ourselves in a better way?*

"*Only to the extent that we expose ourselves
over and over to annihilation can that
which is indestructible in us be found.*"

–Pema Chodron

Invite yourself to do better.

Send yourself an invitation to your own
multilevel marketing pyramid party!

You know, the one that uses love
and personal freedom as its product.

Distribution happens automatically!

115

- Create the environment for others that you want for yourself.

- Our expansion is a quietly noted thing within. We may want to express it to people, however, we can't really tell them. We can only be an example of it. Their recognition of it is for them to see.

- We can always, always, always make small, incremental steps toward something better.

- Sometimes we need to learn things over and over and over and over again until we reset our nervous system enough so we can apply what our minds have downloaded. It can be like eliminating an addiction—we think about shifting away from it over and over until one day we do fully shift, right down to the cellular level.

- If you can't take action now, prepare yourself to take action sometime, and maintain clear intention towards goals of the heart.

Realign yourself toward your truth,
over and over again, until you tap in.
See it, feel it, over and over again, until you become it.

Most people just want to feel a little nicer
than they currently do.

They're not looking for any supreme experience
or huge epiphany shift.

They just want a little more gentleness.

Besides, being just a little nicer eases
the pressure of being completely awesome all the time!

On our journey, we will find ourselves making
incremental, small, sometimes imperceptible steps
toward an often unknown something better.

Beginning
Again,
Redefining
Your Journey

Stay the Path

In life, we're repeatedly gifted with the lessons and opportunities to practice what it is to live outside of fear and live in love, to understand that our fear simply presents us time to choose a different way. And in pointing ourselves toward love, we can then accept what it is to change for the sake of love.

Fear always begs the question: "Can I see this in a new, fresh way?"

Just mentioning the concept of remembering our truth automatically triggers most of us into thinking about the possibility of a greater purpose to our spirited journey. When we're challenged at any level to be with our truth, we have no choice but to start re-exploring ourselves, to begin to think again and differently about who we are, and to explore that precious connection to life's core essence that we tend to forget. In opening more to the forgotten possibilities of love, we find a path to that which we most desire— our peace. This is our challenge in a world that often seems to direct us away from the very thing we most yearn for.

From this point on, the rest of your life
will only be what you make it!

119

Beginning
Again,
Redefining
Your Journey

Part 2

A Metaphor for Our Quality of Thought

When my son, John, was about three years old, I brought him to a local park that had an open field so he could practice riding his bike. I figured it would be safe—it was open, flat, and had a soft blanket of grass covering the whole place. The only obstacle in the entire field was one 4x4 post sticking about four feet out of the ground.

I felt sure I could keep my boy away from it. It was only one post in a large area, and it was all the way on the other side of the field. Being an overly concerned father, I kept yelling to John, "Be careful of the stick in the ground!" And once he got going on his bike, in his excitement, he couldn't stop looking at that 4x4 post. *Look out for the stick! Don't hit the stick! Don't hit the stick, John!* I kept on warning him.

Well, sure as sugar, he couldn't take his eyes off of it. I watched as my sweet little boy, just three years old, rode his bike right into the only obstacle in the park, that 4x4 post. Luckily, he didn't get hurt and we all laughed about it, but there's a moral to the story: Our attention will determine our direction. Don't let the last thing you see be a 4x4 staring you in the face!

Inspirational
Espresso

Creating Quality
of Thought

Thought is the spice that flavors every experience!

Life is already so short.

Don't make it shorter!

In understanding the nature of how thought and the mind work in our lives, we come to realize that we don't have to rely on others for answers to our questions or struggles. By understanding the mind, we get that those solutions very naturally lie within. We don't have to continuously ruminate over our issues to figure out our challenges. Often, it's the process of letting our thinking about these problems settle a bit that allows the solutions a quieter space to present themselves. Our solutions patiently await their recognition behind our frantic thinking. That's just the nature of things.

Just like breathing, thinking happens. Our walk through life, our existence here depends on us understanding the manifestations and consequences of that. The quality of our lives can depend on whether or not we get caught up in the phenomena of being alive in our life, or in the ordeal of trying to grab onto every thought that comes into our head and thinking our way through it. Often, this quality is of our own choosing.

Our thinking can help us create wellbeing, or get in the way of it. It's based in how we use the gift of free will, a gift which only we have control over. Feelings are based in this. Our emotional state is not a reflection of the quality of our lives. It's simply an expression of the quality of our thinking in that moment. It's this that directs the quality of our experience.

The mind is never still and unattached
to any particular thought.
It simply ebbs and flows, not unlike the wind—
sometimes strong, sometimes barely perceptible,
but always, always bringing life.

"I can feel guilty about the past,

apprehensive about the future,

but only in the present can I act.

The ability to be in the present moment

is a major component of mental wellness."

-Abraham Maslow

We all experience a reality dependent upon where we are in our lives. It's our quality of thinking that determines our feelings and our connection with joy or suffering. The thinking we bring to life directs our state of wellbeing at any particular moment.

The quality of thinking we entertain about our reality definitively directs the tone of our journey.

Moment after moment, new life flows forward,

experienced through our awareness of thought.

That's the nature of life.

We will experience life in exactly the same light

that we choose to give life to.

"Life does not consist mainly—or even largely—of
facts and happenings.

It consists mainly of the storm of thoughts
that is forever blowing through one's head."

-Mark Twain

"What we see depends mainly
on what we look for."

-John Lubbock

People like a good fortune cookie because it can help them create power statements for their lives! Who hasn't held onto the fortune cookie fortune for a time just because it had some pizzazz? We embody a bit of strength through it, and it leaves us with a smile and a fresh look at how we might participate with a bit more heart in our world.

The quality of our journey is often dependent
on us finding a freshness in our thought.
Adding a little fortune cookie moxie to our step!

"You are the sky.
Everything else—it's just the weather."

-Pema Chodron

When it comes down to it,
you really have no control over others,
so why would you give them control over you?

Once you understand that it's within your control
to choose the quality of your thinking,
it changes you forever.
You can't forget it.

We tend to get somewhat insecure about things
until we understand them.

Your only limitation in interacting with more love
is your belief that love cannot be present
in those interactions.

We are all graced with the privilege of being able
to choose the quality of our thinking,
and thus we have great influence on our life experience.

Inspirational
Espresso

And who are you, and what quality do YOU choose?

In dark moments,
when suffering feels victorious,
there is a hidden light
ripe for your fresh seeking eyes.

"*Emotions don't reveal the quality of our life,*
they reveal the quality of our thinking
at any particular moment."

–Tommy Newberry

Stuck in unproductive and disruptive thought,
we abandon our life and the moments that yearn
for our awareness.

"*The most difficult times for many of us*
are the ones we give ourselves."

–Pema Chodron, When Things Fall Apart

"*We see the world not as it is,*
but as we are."

–Anais Nin

Any one of us, at any moment, is always one thought
from peace or fear, from being a Gandhi
or thinking like a Hitler.

It's our free will thought that we give life to
and the level of consciousness we cultivate
within that allows this or prevents it.

In the same way we are asked to care for the earth,
we are also the stewards of our minds…

We are the stewards of our thinking.

No one else can be that for us.

Inspirational
Espresso

Truly, what thought
is worth giving up my life to?

For the anxious mind, things are never
exactly what they seem, and anxious thought
is never as real as we give it credit for.
Anxiety's real motivation is to take us away
from our true nature, away from our peace.

After all, what use is there for truth
to the anxious mind?

———————

Life is not about things.
It's about being fully awake to your experiences.

Your car, your money,
your prestige is pointless in this place.

———————

Our quality of thinking
is the pigment in the paint.
Through it we define the color
of our experience in this world.

Your thinking completely determines
your state of wellbeing, and the more you resist that,
the more you welcome anxious states
to own you and your time on this planet.

No matter the situation, simply know:
"I can see this differently if I want to."
This is always an option, an eternally open door.

"The truths we so cling to depend
greatly on our point of view."
–Obi-Wan Kenobi to Luke Skywalker

Inspirational
Espresso

Emotions reflect the quality
of whatever thought you're engaging in.
It's a mistake to believe that those same,
always temporary emotions are reflecting
the quality of your life.

Your state of wellbeing at any moment
is a snapshot of where your thoughts
and thinking are.

Nuts and bolts, bottom line:
We are thinking beings, and all we ever really own
is the thought we walk into the room with.

Creating
Quailty of
Thought

Choosing Thought, Choosing Life, Choosing Love

"We are always only one thought away from peace."

-Sid Banks

Time is a tricky thing. We hold it close and see its precious value, yet it so easily gets lost to us in life's busyness. Step back from the obsessive busyness of living, the whirlpool of past and future thought sloshing through your head, and find your better way. Immerse yourself in this moment that's in front of you, while you have one!

Fragile as life can be, it can shift and change in the blink of an eye for everyone. We are all vulnerable to the unpredictable, often difficult shifting of our lives. In Buddhism there is a quote, "Life is so hard, how can we be anything but kind?" No one is really ever that far away from suffering, so how can we not at least try to show compassion to one another?

Live your life without preconceptions, expectations, manipulations, or obsessive ruminations. Be in your precious moments and embrace your presence in this world—there is life in every breath. The chatter in your head does not want you to get lost in it, but like breathing air or pumping blood, it reminds you that you are alive, so treat it as such.

We often look outside ourselves for things we think will provide us with happiness and higher states of being when, in truth, what we seek already exists within us. We just need to open up and tap into it.

Loving life is not about what you get, but what you give.

How we experience this life is always about the quality of thought and consciousness that we bring into the room. It's our most direct influence on our personal state of wellbeing.

Here's a beautiful example of choosing love from the movie, *Adaptation*.

Charlie Kaufman: There was this time in high school. I was watching you out the library window. You were talking to Sarah Marsh.

Donald Kaufman: Oh, God. I was so in love with her.

Charlie Kaufman: I know. And you were flirting with her. And she was being really sweet to you.

Donald Kaufman: I remember that.

Charlie Kaufman: Then, when you walked away, she started making fun of you with Kim Canetti. And it was like they were laughing at *me*. You didn't know at all. You seemed so happy.

Donald Kaufman: I knew. I heard them.

Charlie Kaufman: How come you looked so happy?

Donald Kaufman: I loved Sarah, Charles. It was mine, that love. I owned it. Even Sarah didn't have the right to take it away. I can love whoever I want.

Charlie Kaufman: But she thought you were pathetic.

Donald Kaufman: That was her business, not mine. You are what you love, not what loves you. That's what I decided a long time ago.

*Choosing
Thought,
Choosing Life,
Choosing Love*

Thought

In Extreme Anxiety (or maybe just a little) ...

Allow yourself to step back and identify that you are caught up in crappy thoughts, and that you need to wait them out and allow them to shift naturally with the understanding that clear thoughts will absolutely become available.

Just keep saying, "It's just thought," and let it pass. Being in a "thought attack" does not define anything about your truth. It just means you're experiencing a distortion of thinking which automatically pulls you away from your true nature of peace and separates you from your inspired wisdom. So leave it be. Allow it to naturally flow away. Understand it is just thought and know that as it flows past, your mind does not have to entertain it. This opens you up to thinking that brings peace and expresses your true nature, your natural wisdom.

Thought is always flowing through the mind. *Always.* Depending on our state of wellbeing at any particular moment, we can attach to the same topic in radically different ways. A frown from someone in the morning can be taken personally, and if held close, can affect your whole day. Or it can be seen through and recognized as coming from a person struggling in his or her own pain and possibly in need of a friend. That spilled cup of coffee can floor us, shame us, anger us, or end in laughter and be shirked off as simply an event that makes us human.

We are all quality control specialists, so pay attention! Tend to the thoughts you wish to produce and bring life to, and do your best to construct your return to peace.

Understanding the nature of thought restores a level of power within. It empowers us to see ourselves more clearly as we interact with life, which in turn, helps us recognize the quality of the thinking we live in. Recognizing our glitches, our distortions in how we're thinking, automatically restores our memory about our power of choice. It isn't always immediate, but always holds the potential of bringing hope and ownership to our experience.

Choosing Thought, Choosing Life, Choosing Love

---

*With free will comes the gift of choice,
asking us to take responsibility for our thinking
and ourselves.*

In every moment, there's always permission
to think differently, to choose something better.

Thought is behind every emotion—good, bad, or neutral.
Our challenge is always one of how
we entertain those thoughts.

Why waste your time in pain
and worry when you could be happy?
The air around you eagerly awaits your new breath.

"I am not bound to win, but I am bound to be true.
I am not bound to succeed, but I am bound to live
by the light that I have."

-Abraham Lincoln

Life brings us plenty of pain and pleasure.
Our responsibility is to define the quality of experience
we prefer to live in and to point ourselves there.

View anxious thinking as temporary noise
passing through your head.
Peaceful thought is the same.
Peace is just nicer, it feels better,
it's more welcoming and congruent with
the truth in our hearts.
It's less a "noise" and more of a melody.

Understanding your fear and anxiety
doesn't give you permission to stay in that fear.
It just opens up the door a crack to let in enough light
so that you can leave when you choose.

Our thoughts are all very real, yet we don't need
to pay attention to every one of them.
Learn discernment and wander toward a gentler way.

Be careful of the thinking you generate around yourself
because in that thinking, you determine
your life experience.

The more you chew on something,
the more you can taste it.
Be careful of what you're biting into
with your thinking.

Inspirational
Espresso

Why cooperate with thoughts
that only want to create suffering?

Reaction is quite automatic and involuntary,
but your choice to respond is yours,
and can never be taken away.

We choose the direction of our thinking, period.

Why make yourself miserable over things
you just ain't got no control over?

"Choose to be optimistic,
it feels better."
—The Dalai Lama

Free will and our use of it
can be our greatest strength or greatest weakness.

Our point of view determines how we use it.

Isn't it comforting to know that there's no thought
that runs through your mind that you absolutely
have to attach to?

Hold yourself back, for just a moment,
from indulging in negative thinking.

You'll find that your world will change for the better.

Inspirational
Espresso

Life

*I wonder if most people know
that they could be happier, stronger, and more at peace.
Do we dare even care to try?*

When we get caught up in difficult moments, we
tend to automatically drop into old negative patterns,
patterns that don't really suit us, don't resonate from
our hearts, but these old ways draw us in through
habit and our familiarity with them. They are our "go
to" behaviors that we automatically default to because
we haven't figured out a better way of approaching
our struggles, at least not yet. All kinds of events
and thoughts can instigate this shifting into our
negativity, stimulate our ill feelings towards ourselves,
others, or the world at large. It commonly happens
when we've somehow ended up feeling less than
about ourselves or inadequate, small, and not enough
at any level. It becomes a place we automatically go to
when we feel our identity or belief systems are threatened, or simply because we have wandered away from
ourselves while in pain and feel separated from our
peace in some way. So we try to avoid our pain by
stepping back into old standby beliefs and paradigms

that create dogmatic attitudes of right and wrong, hold close to assumptions about ourselves and others, participate in old habits of gossip, passive-aggressive behavior, and small, fear-based thinking about ourselves and others. We rekindle a familiar old place within, and we create our very own personal state of hell—until, that is, we recognize the slip and choose a different way. This choice can be difficult and seems to always come at the most inconvenient of times…particularly when we thought we had moved past a specific event or problem. Perhaps we had developed an "I'm done with that" attitude around the issue. So pay attention. When we can recognize that we're stuck in our pain, suffering and subsequent negativity, it's our internal alarm telling us that it's time to reboot ourselves again, to find our way, to step back away from fear and toward love. It may not change anything about a situation except the way you see it, but seeing it with fresh eyes and a new quality of thought, seeing it through love rather than fear, that's enough, that changes it, and most importantly, that changes you.

On this wonderful journey of ours, we are always renewing our walk toward love. Reconnecting with the quality of energy that resonates with our true nature inevitably affects the health of our physical body, right down to the cellular level, our mind, and the quality of the thoughts we entertain, our spirit, and our connection with our spirited essence. Resetting ourselves away from negative patterns revitalizes us on all levels and engages us in a more profound way on our journey, expanding us back toward our true nature. We resonate with truth, with love.

Ironically, the act of participating in the human experience means "being" the experience, being present in it, alive in the moment as best as you are able.

It's not so much about what we do, rather it's about being there, and taken by life when we do it.

We all have times where we get stuck in our self-importance at the expense of living our lives.

"When you die,
you will have unread emails in your inbox."
-Alan Cohen

One moment, one breath, even one half of a breath
of quiet mindfulness, and a gentleness is present within.
You choose to step toward
that place of grounding or you do not.
Being in your breath puts it a little more
within your grasp, a little closer to recognizing
and remembering peace, you get closer
to saying, "Yes."

Inspirational
Espresso

When our thinking
gets in the way of living our lives,
something needs to change.

It takes so much more effort not to love
than to allow peace to germinate.
Our resistance to the change toward love
is what makes opening to love seem so hard.

After all, we take our time when we're cooking,
and we can spend days looking for the perfect office chair
or choosing the right kind of nail polish—why not
attend to the quality of our thinking
with the same enthusiasm?

When we get stuck in thinking that's disruptive
and unnecessary, we lose so many of the life-filled
moments given to us.

Step away and ask yourself:
"Is this thought worth giving up my life for?"

What thought am I willing to give my life for?

That answered: I have nothing to worry about.

Think about it...

(When we're stuck in any negative
or anxious thought, where do we live?)

If you want to move closer to God,
you need to move closer to things of God.
Start with your thinking and the rest of life
takes care of itself.

Inspirational
Espresso

" *L*ife is no brief candle to me.
It is a sort of splendid torch which I have got a hold of
for the moment, and I want to make it burn
as brightly as possible before handing it
onto future generations. "

-George Bernard Shaw

If you have substituted the richness of a heart
for the world's riches,
consider recalibrating.

What is so important in life
that it is worth forgetting ourselves for?

"You will find as you look back upon your life
that the moments when you have truly lived
are the moments when you have done things
in the spirit of love."

—Henry Drummond

Choosing
Thought,
Choosing Life,
Choosing Love

Why ruminate on all those past events
when that's just not who or what you are anymore?
Look instead at who you're becoming.

We periodically need to, or are forced to, remind ourselves
that the final destination on this journey is not one of
"getting there," but one of loving better,
and that's a journey that has no definable end.

When you get to the point where life around you feels like
it's about to collapse or explode,
that there's a turmoil building within you
and you can barely stand it any longer,
no matter what "it" is, pay attention.

You're close to something juicy!

Inspirational
Espresso

Every moment of every day we're choosing our life,
choosing to be either alive and present
to our experience or stuck in our heads.

We acknowledge the brilliant miracle of life
itself or exist in mindless internal chatter
that has no end and gives no comfort.

We feel our world without judgment, or we feel fear.

There's not a middle ground worth striving for here.

Holding our fear "kind of close" and then letting in
"enough love" isn't the answer—we just end up existing
in a self-contrived state of limbo
when we try to negotiate with suffering.

"*That millions share the same forms*
of mental pathology does not
make those people sane."

-Erich Fromm

We can only be present to love, look through and
explore all its facets and influences, all the ways of
love, or we can be swayed into fear, allowing all the
seductive strings that attach with the ways of fear to
bind us and hold our hearts. One cultivates freedom
and reconnects us with our truth, the other maintains
us in a mental and emotional prison of stasis within. We may not always see it immediately, but it's a
choice, it's our choice—no one can visit both terrains

at once. We can't frightfully love anything, and we can't lovingly fear as much as we might argue for the privilege. Embracing one automatically rules out the other.

This choosing of love over fear is the only life choice which holds any enduring meaning, the only choice that directly impacts absolutely everything we do and every direction we take in life. There's always the choice between these two, love or fear. The question persists until we feel its answer. Which do we want to own? Which choice do we want to live? Once again, it's all about you and your heart, this journey of ours.

"Perfect love casts out fear.
If fear exists, then there is not perfect love."
-A Course in Miracles

There is an art to wanting what you already have. An art I don't believe I have perfected yet, but I do keep at it!

Love

"Where there is love, there is life."

-Mahatma Gandhi

"Love liberates, it doesn't bind."

-Maya Angelou

This might just be the most overused story in the history of inspirational writing. It's a story about guiding our internal voice and choosing our thinking, but it's wonderful and absolutely bears repeating...

Choosing Thought, Choosing Life, Choosing Love

Feeding the Wolf

In the Cherokee tradition, the legend of *Two Wolves* depicts our journey between good and evil and accepting full responsibility for how we choose to think and who we choose to be.

Two Wolves speaks of a grandparent passing their wisdom down to their grandchildren—wisdom about the ubiquitous struggle in life, of choice.

As the story goes: The grandchildren were curious about their grandmother, wondering how it was that she always seemed so happy, how she seemed to live with such peace and strength.

She told them that long ago she realized there were two wolves inside of her, each fighting for attention. One was the wolf of fear, anger, resentment, and of all the emotions that created pain for herself and others. The other was the wolf of love, understanding, and kindness, holding the emotions of truth and personal strength. Both wolves were part of her and she could feel them battle for her heart. She could feel their power.

She told her grandchildren, "The two wolves exist in everyone, including you. At one time, I sided with whichever wolf grabbed my attention, feeling joy in one moment and anguish or pain in the next, thinking *I* made the choice, but I was at the mercy of whichever wolf was loudest in me. Then, I realized that the only wolf asking for attention was my angry wolf, the wolf that kept me in tension. I noticed that beauty does not demand attention, and I wanted to live a beautiful life. So even today, over and over again, I make my choice to be in my beautiful life. I choose to feed the wolf of love and compassion. This is why I stand with honor, this is how I know who I am, and this is why I see the beauty that exists within all of my grandchildren. Because I choose to."

She went on, "The wolf of fear does not bring the gifts that make my life worthwhile. It's the wolf of love that allows me to remember my truth and to see the beauty of yours. My wolves never stop fighting, some days are more difficult than others, and the battles can be vicious, but I know how it will end. I always know who will win."

Unable to contain his excitement, the child asks the grandmother, "How do you know which one will win?"

She smiled with her eyes and said, "It's always the wolf that I feed."

Every time I read that story it touches me! We are in charge of feeding our thinking! Thinking simply exists, in all its qualities, this is not our problem. What we give our life to is!

A worthy intention:

**Do anything, every day, to make the world
a better place.**

---

*Trust in your creation,
trust in your healing,
trust in your wisdom,
trust in your love.*

---

*How do we approach people in pain
so that they can better understand their own beauty?
How do we approach ourselves
so that we can recognize and walk with the love
that exists already in our being?*

What is the one-three point?

You're so busy pointing at what other people are doing
that you forget to look back at yourself
in a way that asks: "How am I like them?"
and, "Am I approaching the situation
with compassion or judgment?"
Ask yourself: "Does the arrogance of looking
at another's weakness and painful behavior
close down my ability to see them and
myself with an open heart?"

A love held openly reminds us
of our origin and our destiny.

Choosing
Thought,
Choosing Life,
Choosing Love

You cannot be in your life
and see its glorious beauty
when looking through the smoke generated
by all the emotions of fear.

Sometimes the greatest prayer
we can give another
is to wish them well.

"*It* takes courage to love, but pain through love
is the purifying fire which those who love
generously know.
We all know people who are so much afraid of pain
that they shut themselves up like clams in a shell,
and giving out nothing, receive nothing, and therefore
shrink until life is a mere living death."

–Eleanor Roosevelt

Just choose to:

This is your gift to you.
We don't love just because we want to,
we love because we choose to, and in that choice,
we rediscover ourselves.

Embracing Opportunity

"Out beyond ideas of right and wrong,
there is a field.
I'll meet you there."
–Rumi

As we work through life, there will be stunning moments when we get stopped in our tracks and realize that we've been living our very precious lives in a way that doesn't nurture the passion of who we actually are. It's a hard bed of nails to get comfortable with and a good one to get off of. If you're not on your deathbed when you realize it, be grateful because you have precious time to resurrect a life worthy of who you are, a life embedded in your truth.

We are presented with a multitude of life lessons through our interactions with others and simply by being alive in this world. But what we learn sometimes doesn't stick to the ribs so well—it's kind of a high fiber lesson of life that we easily find ourselves forgetting. So, periodically, softly ask yourself (or scream—whatever!): "Am I paying attention to what the universe wants me to see?" Sometimes we have to create a little enthusiasm within to force ourselves to take another look at the gifts we've been offered—the gifts that help us move toward our love!

Our negative perceptions about what someone else's intentions may possibly be only limits us as we move through our lives. It holds us in a self-constructed world where our fear maintains the bulk of our attention.

When we decide not to take what others do or say personally, or refuse to assume their intentions are bad, it's easier for us to step forward and give everyone, including ourselves, more opportunity to do better, to heal, to love one another.

As much as we hate to admit it, struggle is opportunity knocking at the door, and there are gifts in every wound. Nothing in this world comes toward us that we can't claim as opportunity. It may be hard to see at first, but look for the gifts that come. They want to lead you back to yourself.

Scared to see or express our own vulnerability,
we become prisoners of our programed beliefs
about the very thing we fear, while living our lives
and never questioning how we got there.

We are here to see and know ourselves,
in our strengths and our vulnerability.
How else can we ever expect to ever
really know one another?

There is the concept of reaching out and grabbing life,
and that's a great thing to do.
But letting go enough to let life grab you…then
you're really living!

We've all heard the phrase, "Breathe through it,"
or, "Take a breath."

This is not so much a physical act as it is a spiritual one.

It's us taking an opportunity to reconnect
with a place that's purer.

When someone tells you to, "Take a breath,"
they don't mean that you should just physically inhale air.

They want you to take the breath of
and into the spirit, to reconnect.

The air part is just a reminder.

Recognition, Recognition, Recognition.

Being open to recognizing the quality of our thinking
in the heat of the moment is essential in helping us
see and understand when we're in toxic thought.
It presents us our opportunity to do something different.

Simply put:
Free will affords us the opportunity,
any time, to think differently.

If we don't entertain the possibility that something
very beautiful can exist within and through us,
it makes it very hard to observe
as we explore ourselves or look upon others.

165

Always be ready to embrace the next opportunity
that inevitably lies in front of you,
challenging you to love better.

Embracing
Opportunity

What is there that forgiveness
cannot bring to our hearts?

It allows us to see everyone, including ourselves,
compassionately and with an understanding
that helps us see them more in their innocence.

Forgiveness brings forward all our opportunity for peace.

———

What a shame it would be to die
having gone everywhere except to one's own self.

———

When we can shine light into our blockages
to see them more clearly, we are presented
with an opportunity to heal.

It's a choice to take that step, to step past our pain
and suffering, and toward knowing ourselves.

Recognizing Our Thinking

"At the core of your being is something you were born with, your 'healthy psychological functioning'... It is where your wisdom lies, it is your peace of mind, your common sense, your satisfaction in life, and your feeling of wholeness."

-Richard Carlson

Thoughts exist as a flow of potential, but it's we who give them life in our personalizing minds. With this understanding, it becomes clear that it's up to us to free ourselves and to step forward in life with greater intention, exercising our ability to point ourselves at our truth and our peace. We choose what part of this flow of potential we want to breathe life into. When we do this with understanding and integrity, we create within us a sense of confidence, volition, and clarity to move forward in our journey back to our true selves.

We are all travelers of the soul. Don't let old familiar patterns of self-deception, fear, suffering, and judgment hold you back from your journey to your truth. Take a new, unfamiliar path—the path not defined by ego, but defined by the quiet voice of the soul. These old patterns, though tempting, appear less frequently, with less intensity and for shorter periods of time when we choose to become less tolerant of their influence.

———

"The intuitive mind is a sacred gift
and the rational mind is a faithful servant.
We have created a society that honors the servant
and has forgotten the gift."

–Albert Einstein

———

We tend to see new concepts through old paradigms of thinking. Whether we're resisting trying new foods, exploring new places or activities, or opening to fresh thinking, we often cling to comfort and familiarity at the expense of experiencing new clarity. It somehow helps us feel in control of otherwise confusing situations.

But never mind about being faithful to your old ways.
Embrace the uncomfortable loving in your life—there's
way more potential in it!

Elimination of old thinking can be a struggle.
Patterns will always try to reignite themselves,
however, their potentiality will change as
you become mindful of their influence.

Hint: If you can't breathe with it,
it may not be the right choice for you.

Recognizing
Our Thinking

When you recognize that you have allowed yourself
to believe in fear,
the only way you can turn
is away.

When you have a thought or thoughts that create suffering of any kind, a good thing to say to yourself might be something like, "This is not congruent with who I want to become. This feeling is not something to act on in this moment; I need to wait until I can cultivate some gentleness around this." If that doesn't work for you, create something for yourself that does, something that helps you create more peace.

Recognizing our distortion, anguish, and suffering
around any particular subject
opens us to an opportunity for the quality
of thought about that subject to change.

We can then know that if we choose,
we can see it from a new, different perspective.

The trick is recognition.
New thought is always poised to step forward
as you let go of suffering.
That's where we find ourselves.
The trick is recognizing all the many subtleties
of your suffering.

We know that we are much more than our pain, more than our suffering, more than our anxious thinking, our fear. We already know that we can experience our lives more centered and in our love, more peaceful and connected to our truth, in a place where our true nature is freer to flow forward, allowing us to unabashedly embrace our precious life. And this, this can be where our day begins and ends—it only requires choice.

Recognizing
Our Thinking

Try not to get stuck in believing that your past experience defines who you are now, or it will covertly become your present experience.

When we're struggling, we're just having
a momentary experience in our head.
Try not giving that experience too much
unwarranted meaning.
Try not to take yourself so seriously.

It's tempting to nurture
our old familiar ways,
but not necessarily productive
in our search for fresh thought.

"The mind can make a heaven out of hell
or a hell out of heaven."

-John Milton

Old behavior is just that—our old behavior.
You may immediately see it, or you may not,
but deep down there is always a hint
of recognition because it always feels
somehow disruptive to your wholeness.

When old disruptive ways whisper,
as they will, pay them no mind.

Once you get the picture of what peace can be,
remember how seductive old ways are
so that you can be prepared for the gymnastics
of the ego and the temptations of the mind.

Recognizing
Our Thinking

Bad choices are often only projections of the fear
that we hold close to our hearts,
with the mistaken belief that our fear was our truth.

Getting Unstuck

"The greatest discovery of any generation is that a human being can alter his life by altering his attitude."
-William James

We can all get stuck in thinking that does not serve our passion. Believing in a memory, made up assumption, or fear requires our heart's attention. It cultivates a thought process that feels all-consuming and all-important, keeping us looking toward something that more resembles a lie that we choose to believe and away from our truth, away from our peaceful selves.

Recognize the moment of personal forgetfulness and choose again.

Go back toward passion, truth, go back to your authentic heart.

We are all yearning to return to our space within,

where peace, not anxiety, waits.

Getting stuck can sometimes be a small, barely perceptible experience. It can be just enough to keep you mildly off balance or miffed for no apparent reason. Or, in a more extreme way, it can explode with all its fanfare as an all-consuming free-for-all expression of dysfunction that puts you over the edge and makes you feel like you're diving into the pond of insanity.

Being stuck in our distracted thinking is quite an individual experience—everyone feeling the same pain in their own way, but whether we are stuck-little or stuck-big, the recognition of our being "in that place again" is the first beautiful step toward healing the pain of being pulled away from our truth and strength. When we're looking away from our heart's truth for any reason, subtle or blatant, it *is* painful to us. Sometimes it just takes a little time to see it.

How do we step toward recognizing when we are out of step? It takes a scientific mindset and a willingness to open up to our imperfection, and to understand that there is always room in any situation to do better. We need to be willing to be wrong—almost thrive on it—because that's the only way we're going to give ourselves the opportunity to see where we're stuck, and in that, we find the opportunity to shift into something better.

When we recognize our limiting thoughts,
it creates understanding we cannot easily ignore.

"Take risks.
If you win, you will be happy.
If you lose, you will be wise."

-Anonymous

We're either suspended in our thought
or headed in a clearer direction.

Refuse to live in that prison of your own construction.

Bash out a brick so you can see the stars!

It's one or the other—you're either in your head
or in your life.

———

We are stuck when we are unable
or unwilling to move toward
a more loving way.

———

"When one door of happiness closes, another opens,
but often we look so long at the closed door
that we do not see the one that has been opened for us."

- Helen Keller

———

Being stuck in your problem only disrupts
the peaceful solution.

Understand this:
The harder we hold on to our thinking,
the more alive and solid it appears to us,
and subsequently, the more easily
it can shroud our truth.

Don't get stuck in someone else's journey.
You'll end up missing your own!

People get stuck in their old, unproductive ways
and don't want to change, but the reality is
that when we allow ourselves to open to new ways,
it gives us the opportunity to see ourselves
more clearly and perhaps become more of
who we really are.

Here, we are given the chance
to acknowledge our truth.

Getting
Unstuck

We can be so busy arguing with one another
and wanting to be right that it destroys
our perspective of common sense and
our compassion for one another.

"Better than a thousand hollow words
is one word that brings peace."

–The Buddha

When fear grabs hold,
clear thought is unattainable.

Your Cousin "It"

- Be willing to recognize it. *(The "it" is anything that pulls you away from your peace.)*

- When you can recognize it, you can walk with it.

- When you can walk with it, you can be with it.

- When you can be with it, you can heal with it.

- When you can heal with it, you can release any need for it.

- When you can release it, you can be free to love it, and yourself.

181

Getting
Unstuck

A Breath
of Patience

"If you're really listening, if you're awake to the poignant
beauty of the world, your heart breaks regularly.
In fact, your heart is made to break;
its purpose is to burst open again and again
so that it can hold evermore wonders."

-Andrew Harvey

Our inclination is to relentlessly search
for the good within us all.
Allow yourself space to be with that.

Our journey walk is one of quiet listening, opening to
the opportunities of knowing a gentle wisdom whispering in our hearts. We absolutely recognize that love
song of the heart because it feels so familiar, so good!

It's quietly known by all, and has the seductive scent of peace on its breath.

Love always feels good, and it comes with celebration. It's a sort of homecoming every time we give ourselves permission to recognize our ability to cultivate love and live it. When we settle into loving ourselves freely, in this moment, we step forward in our walking world, often in a new, very different way. We see ourselves, our thinking, and those around us with a different focus and with fresh eyes. Nothing ever again looks or feels as it did.

Open to the journey of settling. Settling into truth, settling toward love, settling into remembering your purpose, and spirited living. You can't force it or intellectualize it. It's just allowing life to be with an open heart.

*The art of a more peaceful life
is knowing when, how, and if we should
respond to our environment.*

When we allow ourselves to mindfully feel and be in
our vulnerability, it gives us a place to choose from.

It allows us to ask the questions necessary for us
to determine and participate in the
healthiest of responses:

How do I step forward from here?

In my truth, what is my best choice?

Choice is always a response
and never a reaction.
Careless reaction sucks the choice
from your heart.

A Breath of
Patience

The situations we find ourselves in
are often not as important as we might think.
What is important is the quality in which we choose
to address them.

When careless attachment to our thinking
gets in the way of living our lives,
something needs to change.
It takes far more effort to decide not to love
than to allow peace to germinate.
Our resistance to that change
is what makes it so hard.

In our quiet moments, we can all find ourselves desiring something more of this life. We may not know exactly what it looks like, but we get that we'll know it when we see it. We sense that there's more than what we're experiencing, and that there's a root reality that exists within us—a reality beyond words that asks us to keep stepping forward toward our insatiable desire to know life. To do this is to explore our hope, our truth, and ourselves.

Inspirational
Espresso

Toxic thinking always makes
our experience more complicated.

Meditation can be as simple as sitting quietly and un-
derstanding that you are alive right now!

Every sensation that you become aware of, no matter
what it is, reinforces your awareness of the amazing life
that you get to be in!

Inspiration does not come easily to the fearful mind.
It asks us for quiet inattention to our troubled thinking
and for our openness in unmasking the gentle scent
of letting our lives be.

Step away from your noisy self.

Be quiet for just a moment and observe as the spirit
makes its attempt to fill you.

There is no Earth-bound description, no ready-bought
manual to tell you what it looks like to be aware.

Simply listen beyond the ears, see beyond the eyes,
and feel beyond the skin.

Remember your experience of existence, of living.

Sometimes it's better to let the snow globe settle
a little bit before we speak.

"Courage doesn't always roar.
Sometimes courage is the quiet voice
at the end of the day saying,
'I will try again tomorrow.'"

-Mary Anne Radmacher

We tend to get somewhat insecure about things
until we understand them.
So step back, wait it out,
welcome yet-to-be-known understanding.
It will change the way you see things.

Inspirational
Espresso

Meditation is not an absence of thinking
but an absence of our attachment to our thinking.
In it, we allow our thinking to be another part
of the flow of life, helping us to rest rather
than fight through it.

Meditation fosters the construction
of the internal framework which allows us
to remember how to be with ourselves,
to be in our truth, and connect with our wisdom,
thus bringing us back to our gentle way within.

189

...everybody can hear the music, if they listen...
*...**everybody** can hear the music, if they listen...*

Be grateful for the partner who helps you
remember who you are,
*especially when they **annoy** you.*

Your second chance is always
right in front of you.

Not all gifts come wrapped up nice and pretty.
Do your best to receive life graciously.
In moments when things seem difficult,
it may not seem like there's much to celebrate,
but there is always a gift to be had, and often,
the greatest part of the gift lies in your reception of it.

Everyone puts in front of us
the peace-filled gifts of life lessons.
They may look other than "peace-filled,"
but be sure, they all hold gifts.

Quiet solitude can help us open to a deeper,
clearer understanding of our journey.

We're sent to one another with profound purpose
running far deeper and more pervasive
than intellectual understanding allows.

It must be sensed from within, felt through our hearts.

And in the quiet moments, when we listen,
sometimes we can nearly capture that light with words,
and we can cop a satisfying smile at our own craftiness.

"Bedeviled, human, your plight,
in waking, is to choose from the words
that even now sleep on your tongue,
and to know that tangled among them
and terribly new is the sentence that
could change your life."

-Marie Howe, The Meadow

A Breath of
Patience

Everybody has a different set of paradigms
that influence them in their personal walk.

They use them and believe in them as true
until they don't need paradigms anymore,
and then, they know their love
is the only system necessary.

There is a truth already present inside,
a knowing that we always feel
but may not always understand.

Inspirational
Espresso

Coming back to spirit, "getting it,"
can feel like a far more solid experience
in our mind-heart connection.
Suddenly, there can be new words that come forward
and help us describe this reunion with our truth.

Sometimes it's a struggle finding
that deeper place within
where you can hear the music
of who you really are.
Be patient with your process.
It's all there inside of you,
waiting for your discovery,
waiting for the reunion.

Anxiety and stress can only survive
with our permission and acceptance.

Sometimes the most compassionate thing
you can do for people is to allow them to go
through the growth process that their spirit is trying
to guide them through.

Don't fool yourself—sitting quietly
with intention is movement.

" If you understand,
things are just as they are;
if you do not understand,
things are just as they are."

–Zen Proverb

When you talk about your problems
and you believe in their fear,
it feels like a burden you're holding on to tightly.

Lighten your grip...

Don't crush the beautiful dove
that you've forgotten to notice in your hand.

So long as you're anxiously attached to the problem,
a solution has little space to present itself.

A Breath of
Patience

Questioning
the Journey

"Unless you walk out into the unknown, the odds of making a profound difference in your life are pretty low."
-Tom Peters

When you start questioning the truth or quality of your thinking and how it impacts your life experience, it puts you in a position to change your thinking patterns. Questioning our thought takes volition, it involves taking on a position of personal strength that encourages us to take charge of our world in a way we may not have done previously.

Questioning thought naturally becomes an act of personal purification, helping us shift our perspective about the quality of thought as it relates to suffering and ego. We move our thinking process from one that can be more fear-based or negative, one that darkens our experience of life, and with volition, we transform it into a quality of thought that encourages the acknowledgment of something better. It might be a yet unknown better or one where we know we're cultivating our truth and personal strengths *within*.

Inspirational
Espresso

The Art of Knowing Better

"Knowing better" can erupt in a miraculous kind of way that surprises its participants with wisdom and a common sense not always easily accessible when we're stuck in ill will of any kind. It's a spark from within, moving outward into our actions, an epiphany of change, a shift away from old paradigms and dogmas that no longer work, all for the sake of living in more love. Knowing better is simply the difference between knowing something from the heart or knowing it from the mind. It may start in the mind as an attempt to understand the confusion of life, but its grand finale always takes place in the heart, and our full embrace of doing better is dependent on that finale. We cannot own "better" until "better" is known from within.

I commonly tell my kids and the students in my clinic that the most important part of learning any subject is being sensitive to knowing what you don't know. There's an art to knowing how to recognize what you're weak in or don't have a grasp of. There's a skill to identifying when you don't know and owning the meaning of a word or how to use a concept or equation. It's an invaluable asset in life, determining what gaps need to be filled in order to understand anything more thoroughly, including ourselves.

If we don't understand an idea and we're unaware of our misunderstanding, we can end up mindlessly skimming over subjects and concepts without taking the needed time to question ourselves. We fail to notice the hints of what we might be missing, to know if we're fully comprehending what's in front of us. And in this moment of not understanding better, we unintentionally set ourselves up to stumble rather than succeed in our endeavors.

Mastering the art of knowing also rings true when we embark on our journey of living this life through the concepts of the heart—when we strive to live from a better place, a more peace justified place. The skill of knowing better often seems like it requires struggle or a certain amount of pain to motivate its awakening. This is often a matter of finding the gifts within the struggle. We unintentionally cultivate an awareness and understanding of where we went wrong and where we can do better through our pain, if we listen. There are lessons in the anguish of regret and wisdom in admitting our mistakes, wishing that we could give our experience another go. Do so with love, try again with more love, because however that might look, this is the journey.

So can we know our better way, our more loving way, before we're forced to go through the suffering? Perhaps. Perhaps not. But the goal is not to avoid pain, because that's impossible. The goal is to learn from it, which is a thoroughly attainable goal.

In living *in* life and getting to a place where deep within our hearts we know better, we have learned how to function from love. We can step back and see that it's similar to knowing and owning any particular subject matter. We need to fully comprehend what it is to grasp and live in our right words, actions, and deeds. We need to own what it is to live in a life saturated in truth, based in love. It's often a slippery road to get there, especially when a particular subject is surrounded with pain, fear, or suffering. Nonetheless, working the art of knowing better is an important path to walk on our journey toward truly doing better.

How hard is it to nurture yourself,
to surround yourself with the same love
that you would like to give to those
you care for and adore?

We need to continually challenge ourselves about the
quality of thinking behind our choices while holding the
intention of creating opportunities to move forward and
into new and better ways of being.

If we never ask questions regarding how we're doing,
moving in any direction becomes limited at best.

"There is nothing either good or bad,
but thinking makes it so."

-William Shakespeare

One of the first and most important steps we can take in
our own minds is questioning (and quieting)
the authority fear has in our lives.

When we take this step toward something more,
we become aware of our process and our journey,
making only ourselves responsible for our wellbeing
and our state of mind.

When difficult thinking arises, ask yourself:

- Am I willing to give my life for this thought?

- Am I willing to spend what precious moments I
  have entertaining this quality of thinking?

- Then take a seat, and for just one quiet moment,
  allow yourself to shift to a softer place within as
  you explore your answers.

Question your thinking,

your assumptions,

your personalized,

habitual,

comfortable,

mind chatter.

Is it worthy of giving your life to?

Does it merit your cultivation?

———————

Live in the questions of this life.

What is my better way to be at peace with those

I struggle with?

*Questioning
the Journey*

———————

Question yourself.

Define the parameters of who you are.

Perhaps one of the most potent questions
you can ask yourself:
Who would you be if your thinking matched your heart?

Within this question lies many of the answers
to inner peace, answers to be remembered.

Who would you be if your thinking matched your heart?
It's kind of a trick question because
to answer it we don't always need to use words.
It tends to get answered with a feeling
as soon as we hear the question.
We feel that immediate connection with a truth
that exists in our heart.
It gets answered and we immediately
see the light that we are.

Inspirational
Espresso

How much of our anxious thinking
is distraction attempting to make our separation
from truth and love more bearable,
at least for a moment?

"A prudent question is one-half of wisdom."

-Francis Bacon

Can you be in your life and see each moment as perfect,
exactly what you need, the perfect situation
to catapult you into remembering that you are
more than the situation?
This is your journey, remembering.

What do I need to experience in order
to remember my beautiful, true self?

Questioning
the Journey

Rumi asks us, "And you?
When will you begin that long journey into yourself?"

Are you on your journey?

There are infinite ways for us to touch the awareness of being on our journey. The first and easiest is by answering the question, "Are you alive?" If you're alive, you're automatically on the journey! It's an easy in!

In our journey, if we're paying attention, we naturally become aware of how often we drop into different forms of distraction. We step back and watch ourselves in toxic thought, addictions of any kind, judgment gossip—any kind of crummy thinking toward others or ourselves. Questioning our thinking is always a form of quality control for the heart. No matter how you integrate it into your journey, it's always about becoming awake to your life. It's all about honoring the journey.

Some mindful quality control hints:

- Be willing to recognize your slips into negative or somehow distorted thought, to see when you are away from your truth. And then be willing to do your work, to do what it takes to right yourself, like you would a tipped over boat; to reset your state of personal wellbeing in whatever way brings true peace.

- Here's a good one! It's just pure wisdom to know when to shut up! Stepping back and observing within rather than jumping into attack mode can allow us to breathe through and respond well to even the toughest problems. So, allow yourself the grace of knowing when to be quiet!

- It's good to not allow ourselves to be completely guided by our anger, anxiety, or fear of any kind. Listen to these feelings, and learn from and respond to them, but living your life through them only creates more of the same. So open yourself to the lessons behind your emotions rather than giving in to being owned by the emotion.

It's a profound question to ask yourself:
"What would you do in this moment,
and who do you become in the absence of fear?"

This question holds the juice of life.
It explodes in the heart.
Its creation is a freedom from everything
that limits the expression of our truth.
Without the influence of pointless fear,
we become a clearer reflection of our truth.
It creates space for light to enter our being,
and for us to find our freedom.
Without fear limiting the mind, we evolve back into
ourselves, becoming again as we are meant to be.
And that becomes all we need in our precious
return to peace.

Questioning
the Journey

Part 3

Marge Weippert

"According to the Talmud,
every blade of grass has its own angel
bending over it, whispering, "Grow, grow."

-Barbara Brown Taylor

Every time Marge graced our office it was like a traveling circus walking through the front doors. She was towering at 4'11", a woman in her mid-seventies with a gently mischievous smile and always an interesting new age-y comment or story to be told (like: "All the birds wanted to sleep with me last night—you could tell the moon was full!" Or, "I almost burnt down the house yesterday making beeswax ear cones," or how she almost burnt her house down again trying to make healing salves. Or how she was using energy work to keep the bugs away from her blueberry fields and how she astro-projected over her land to make sure everything was okay).

Marge was always wearing some kind of authentic 1960s purple flowing dress, sparkly purple and indigo blouse, a large and very ornate hat with feathers from her own personal Amazon parrots, and large earthy jewelry. She would inevitably lay down on the table for an adjustment and giggle that she had neglected to wear any underwear that day. She was quite an endearing, quirky character, and that is putting it lightly. Never a dull moment, and always, always, always on the fringe of rational thinking.

I was working with Marge in the clinic one day and feeling kind of judgmental about who she was. I started thinking to myself, "You are so odd, always thinking so differently, talking about energy *this* and vibration *that*, always into all these odd little fringe practices that the average, 'normal' person never even thinks about. Marge, you're really, really weird," I said to myself. As soon as I had that thought, my own oddities flashed in front of me. They were really no different in their fringe quality than Marge's. I was just as much of an oddity, just as much of a strange little human as Marge—a free soul in my own way, just like Marge. I heard a little voice in my head say, "You are Marge, and Marge is you," and in that moment, I took a breath because I knew that this was the truth of it. No one is really that different from everyone else in this world. Marge and I were different, but in such a profound way, exactly the same. We were both as human as you get, doing our best based on the experiences we had lived through so far and approaching life based on our understanding of them.

In that moment, when I knew we were the same, I knew that, like me, all she wanted was love and compassion, and she wanted the freedom to give the same. So that's what I gave her from that point on, never judging her so harshly again. We had a wonderful, always interesting relationship until she passed. It was a gift for both of us.

Marge
Weippert

Seeing the Miracle

"Whoever you are, you are human.

Wherever you are, you live in the world,

which is just waiting for you

to notice the holiness in it."

–Barbara Brown Taylor, An Altar in the World:
A Geography of Faith

As we remember the truth of ourselves,

we are able to see with infinite depth

into our own soul.

All Are Miracles within Miracles

How would it change the rest of your life if in every moment you knew that you were fully immersed in a miracle—if you walked in that knowing, as often as you were able, how might that change you? How would it be knowing that every breath you take is a miracle, that every thought, every emotion, every movement you contemplate and make choices in, every little moment of aliveness you experience is a huge, juicy miracle? Who would you be if you walked with that core of understanding constantly influencing you? How would you be? How might that change your awareness of being alive?

Can you wander in your mind and open
to an understanding that perhaps
what's in front of all of us right now
has manifested through a precious and
mystical breath of guidance and wisdom?

And though we may not have the capacity to grasp
the meaning of our path in this moment,
our only need may be to accept it.

"There comes a time when the mind
takes a higher plane of knowledge
but can never prove how it got there."

-Albert Einstein

There's purpose behind everything with reasons
that are beyond what we can know.

Our moments, whether difficult or beautiful,
are pieces of a bigger, more infinite puzzle
we may never fully comprehend.

Seeing the
Mircale

When times are dark, it can help to remember
that this life, despite its suffering,
Is Indeed Miraculous.

We originate in and operate from
a formless flow of infinite energy.
Our wisdom and truth naturally unfold
through us endlessly.

"Realize ordinary life is an unbroken
flow of normal miracle."
-Andrew Harvey, Return of the Sacred Mother

When all is said and done in life,
we're meant to sit in admiration of our
own beauty and the beauty that surrounds us.
Inspired, we suddenly see the amazing truth
of our existence and we can't help but feel
that which is beyond our ability to speak.

We sit in stunned silence as we feel the beauty
of who we are within this miraculous creation,
and in that feeling we simultaneously become
aware of the infinite complexity and infinite simplicity

that we've been graced with.

We come to know that our journey back to ourselves
is an eternal and sacred one,
overwhelmingly beautiful to the mind
and stunningly familiar to our heart.

Your world can be seen as the miracle of life
happening around you or as chaos.

It's always **your** *choice.*

A miracle is an event inexplicable by any natural or
scientific laws we know of…yet.

Seeing the
Mircale

Doesn't everybody find it unbelievably amazing that
we even exist?!!!

"There are only two ways to live your life.

One is as though nothing is a miracle.

The other is as though everything is a miracle."

–Albert Einstein

Ineffable: When you cannot find adequate words to describe something's profundity.

in•ef•fa•ble

/in-ef-*uh*-b*uh* l/

Adjective

Too great or extreme to be expressed or described in words: "Ineffable beauty."

Too sacred to be uttered.

Inspirational
Espresso

How much of life actually falls into this category of breathtakingly ineffable? When you stop and feel it, when you look with your heart and are really absorbed into it, everything can leave you stunned into silence. When you're awake, everything about life is an ineffable experience.

Synonyms: unspeakable - inexpressible - unutterable - nameless

Are we not all ineffable miracles?

Every moment we spend in the past or the future, we are spending away from the present and most precious moment—living life away from recognizing the miracle.

Oh, how our universe has conspired to create us virtually out of nothing and into a miraculous being of infinite possibilities!
How could this be if not by the hand of one that's equally as infinite?!

Seeing the Mircale

This world is pure miracle—how can everything not be infinitely interrelated?

"When you are here and now, sitting totally,
not jumping ahead, the miracle has happened.
To be in the moment is the miracle."

−*Osho*

This life is an infinitely organized coincidence,
with coffee.

There is so much more to realize of this world,
and so much to distract us away from it.

Inspirational
Espresso

Try not to miss the miracle of what is in front of you.

Healing Opportunities, Exploring Gifts in the Wound

"People say that what we're all seeking
is a meaning for life.

I don't think that's what we're really seeking.
I think that what we're seeking is an experience
of being alive, so that our life experiences
on the purely physical plane will have resonance
within our own innermost being and reality,
so that we actually feel the rapture of being alive."

-Joseph Campbell

Sometimes the greatest obstruction to our healing
is being stuck in the fear that we may never heal.

We forget that our bodies are made to heal,
every tissue and cell we have is programmed
to recognize disruption, search for balance,
and regenerate.

And it doesn't stop with the body.

Body, mind, and spirit—we are made to heal.

Oh, how we chew on the stitches!

As we strive to make sense of our wounds, and we all have many, we can end up dwelling on them, chewing them up to no avail, over and over again in our heads. The resulting scenario is that we end up surrounded with the same thought process that we started with, and we create a neurological pattern of seeing ourselves as victims of circumstance. That rumination becomes the tool of our own self-inflicted suffering. The initial issue may not have been in our control, but the way we revisit and relive it is.

All of our wounds are time irrelevant—they are in the past as soon as they happen. Do not hold them close.

We are asked to see our wounds as gently and compassionately as we can with the intention of healing. They bring many gifts with their pain, including the gifts of contrast and compassion: "I hurt, therefore I wish not to be the cause of hurt." When we step past our suffering and search for whatever lesson can be learned, we live in the solution and not the problem. Be love rather than fear.

As the Buddhists say,
"Without pain, no compassion."

There is a vastness to this life experience
we may never fully grasp.

Marcia is my longtime friend and office manager. Sadly, her mother, Cora, passed away in October of 2015, a month from the writing of this story. She tripped on the stairs, severely hurt her wrist, knee and neck, and struggling with the injuries, her heart just couldn't or didn't want to take any more. As wonderful fate might have it, everyone had about ten good days with her in the hospital, blessed that she was conscious and clear. Her last breath was quiet, like her demeanor, and she passed at about three in the morning on a Friday.

Healing
Opportunities,
Exploring
Gifts in the
Wound

Marcia called me and let me know at about 5:30am and started her process of understanding. I started out early that morning, before traffic or people were moving much, and walked up toward town for coffee at 6:00am. I was thinking about Marcia and her struggle, and just as I was walking past the Bookman, our local bookstore, I heard her mom's voice in my head say, "I didn't realize it would be this big." Now, Cora barely said anything to me in life so I was more than a little surprised when I heard from her afterward, and the sensation I felt coming from her was one of pure expansion, freedom, and happiness. My mind went right to all those spirits that were so pleasantly surprised when they willingly stepped forward on the journey of transition, embracing whatever newness was in front of them, so happy to be free. It was very comforting.

I had been thinking about death recently—I'm sure it has to do with being fifty-four years old and watching people begin to leave this plain. My experience with Cora took the charge off of death for me. Quite a gift from a woman I've hardly ever talked to.

Our acceptance of life and death yields similar experiences. In death, when we throw acceptance and love into the mix, we expand to places beyond understanding, beyond what we can know, and when we throw fear into the mix, death becomes a contracting experience, an experience of feeling eternally stuck. It's very similar to our acceptance or resistance to our lives.

But with death, it seems like the experience is on steroids. It's just a thought, I don't know yet...

We often reopen our wounds,
using any tools necessary,
until we no longer have a need to do that surgery,
until we find a better way to be alive in our lives.

When we talk about things of the heart,
people shift.
They get it and yearn for this kind
of loving communication.
It's impossible for this not to happen on some level,
even if we can't always see it.

Healing Opportunities, Exploring Gifts in the Wound

Look for the gift in the wound. There are always hidden gifts in our wounds, we just need to open up to their presence and explore their secret message.

We have all been somehow wounded,
and within every wound lay gifts of understanding
and compassion.

You can only be effective in your life
when you are affected by your life.

It's not that there's anything wrong with you.
It's just that sometimes you have a hard time
seeing what's right.

My desire is always to help create
the opportunity to heal.

We love our world by helping to create
opportunities of healing.

Whether it be hearts, minds, bodies, the land,
air or water, loving healing is essential
for our wellbeing and our survival.

We are simply asked to participate.

---

*"Once I gave up the hunt for villains,
I had little recourse but to take responsibility
for my choices.
Needless to say, this is far less satisfying
than nailing villains.
It also turned out to be more healing in the end."*

-Barbara Brown Taylor

---

*When you believe that someone is different from you,
that you need to provide them with
more of your critical judgment,
believing that in some way they are a threat to you
and that they need to be taken personally,
then not very suddenly or subtly at all,
you no longer can find your own peace within,
so forget about having it with anyone else.*

*Healing
Opportunities,
Exploring
Gifts in the
Wound*

If we ask for healing around our suffering,
we become open to the understanding
that we are an integral part of our own healing.

As soon as we refer to our suffering as pain,
we create for it a new identity that inspires that healing.

Because in our pain, we look for the lesson presented
and seek healing, but in our suffering,
we submerge ourselves in our mental anguish
and only see that same suffering.

It's all semantics, but it's a worthy insight to understand.

The body heals and you're its partner.

In being of service to others,
we will recognize ourselves.

"We don't set out to save the world.
We set out to wonder how other people are doing
and to reflect on how our actions affect
other people's hearts."

-Pema Chodron

Whatever your injury, addiction, or suffering
may look like, believe that you can heal,
that you were made to heal.

In our discomfort with the difficult past events
in our lives, we may be saying to ourselves,
"What I really want is to forgive myself for that issue."
Maybe this is the healing we are all looking
for—self-forgiveness.

Healing
Opportunities,
Exploring
Gifts in the
Wound

Disrupted thinking takes a willing participant.

Clarity requires the same.

Recognizing that we're stuck presents us
an opportunity to step back and see ourselves
more clearly and with a compassionate eye.
This act creates an opportunity for healing.

Inspirational
Espresso

There are unknown and unexpected influences
that guide us in our healing, infinite in their nature
and persistent in their goal.
Thank goodness!

Everything needs to heal in its own time.
Each new understanding we embrace is a building block
for the next step in our journey.

*It is one of the many incremental stepping stones
back toward ourselves.*

*As we evolve, we pass into and through numerous
experiences and explorations of ourselves,
each allowing us to remember what was forgotten,
and to remember with greater clarity
that which we have always been.*

Everything needs to heal in its own time.

*No two people heal exactly the same
or have exactly the same wound.
We are all different and we all heal in ways
that are individual to ourselves.
Therefore, our only requirement
is patience with our journey.*

*Healing
Opportunities,
Exploring
Gifts in the
Wound*

*There is a quietness I seek
that requires nothing
but me being present in my life.*

Our bodies work as sensitive barometers
to let us know how we're doing on our journey.
High pressure, low pressure—the body responds.
We, in our very essence, are truth meters!

Inspirational
Espresso

We Are All
Journey Friends

*"I am a human being
and nothing human can be alien to me."*

-Maya Angelou

Infinitely the Same

We all hear the same message, but we just have different ears. Everybody hears, feels, experiences the essence of their truth in a way that is individual to them. What's the point in arguing about the words around it? It's the feelings that exist within each of us that we understand. The words can be pretty confusing (which makes sense for something that has no words to express it).

I love the concept that no two people will have exactly the same experience when it comes to their personal insight of what they consider God to be. I can seek God exactly the same as another, and even understand and see spirit the same, using similar words to explain it, and yet each of us feel the presence of spirit in ways that only we feel it. No two people will use the same path or have exactly the same experience.

There are seven billion people in the world, and seven billion ways to see God. We all look at the same spirited beauty from an angle that we have made individually ours.

*Our differences are not so much in the spirit
but lay in the breath of our personal experiences
and the complexity of our physical form
and the meaning that we place on them,
but spirit doesn't see these things.*

Seeing one another as absolutely no different
on the inside, in spirit, no different
in the essence of who we are, has the beautiful
potential of helping us better embrace one another,
especially in the quality of our thoughts.

It opens us up to not take the behavior of others
so personally and helps us find peace with everyone
because we can see them as ourselves, and in that,
understand them in their more spiritual innocence.

Use your life and what happens in it to cultivate compassion for others.

Every emotion, every pain, every difficulty, every moment of being judged and feeling bad can be used in a creatively loving way to find compassion for those who have experienced the same. We are all in the same boat of life, and in this journey, if you can become a little gentler and see things from the perspective of others, it allows you to cultivate a strength within to walk with and love better with.

We Are All
Journey
Friends

Sometimes the most compassionate thing
you can do for someone is to allow them
to go through the growth process their spirit
is trying to guide them toward.

The metta sutta meditation is a Buddhist sermon on unconditional love which encourages maintaining the beautiful attitude of goodwill toward all beings, no matter who they are or what they've done, believing that it's the source of personal happiness and the end to suffering:

May I/you be at peace

May I/you feel safe

May I/you feel happy

May I/you feel strong

May I/you live with ease.

Recite this to yourself—for you, for others—with the intention of maintaining an attitude of goodwill toward all beings, no matter who they are or what they've done.

When we cultivate a higher state of consciousness within,
it creates interest and curiosity,
and it will draw the same out of others
so they can experience it for themselves.

Just like you,
everyone's entitled to their glitches.

Understand that you are not alone.

We all experience life in pretty much the same way.

Pain and anxiety are common among
even the most spiritual.

The only question anyone really needs to ask
themselves is:

Can I do better?

*We Are All
Journey
Friends*

"*Human potential is the same for all.*

Your feeling, 'I am of no value,' is wrong.

Absolutely wrong.

You are deceiving yourself.

We all have the power of thought—so

what are you lacking?"

-Dalai Lama

We are all authorities on being;
our existence in human form makes us so.

You don't need to study how anybody else's mind works.

You just need to understand your own.

In that understanding,
you will see and know how others' function.

Open your eyes.

Look up.

Look down.

No one is above you, no one is below you.

*Believing that we are separated from our truth
or from each other naturally and quite automatically
results in a fear-based reality.*

*Your thinking about others should roughly equate
to the way you would like others to think about you,
if you were them.*

Now there's a pickle for you to figure out!

"We are all meant to shine, as children do.
We were born to make manifest the glory
of God that is within us.

It is not just in some of us; it is in everyone.

And as we let our own light shine,
we unconsciously give other people permission
to do the same.

As we are liberated from our own fear,
our presence automatically liberates others."

-Marianne Williamson

Our most profound feelings of the heart
are the result of seeing beyond our physical lives
and forgiving our past mistakes and missteps
so that we can peer into our own beauty—and
with that, we can open ourselves to the perfect beauty
that exists in everyone, beyond imperfections.

We can have perfect moments,
but perfection lives in imperfection.
Our inevitable mistakes give our spirit something to
do—and boy, do we keep them busy!

Shih nih bi-teen.
"Mind my road."

"A blanket must have an outlet...a mere
thread of a different color or a slight,
apparently accidental break in the border pattern,
which looks like an imperfection.
But if it were omitted, the woman might
get the blanket sickness and lose her mind."
(Navajo adage)

Traditional Navajo blankets and rugs, for which the Navajo are famous, are always created with an intentional imperfection woven into a corner, a purposeful flaw. Interestingly enough, this flawed area is where the Navajos believe "the Spirit moves in and out of the piece." Likewise, our imperfections allow our spirit to move into, out of, and through our lives in a dynamic, symbiotic way. And we, just like a Navajo rug, can be seen as perfectly imperfect. And just like a Navajo rug, we are made to have spirited energy flowing in and through us.

Cultivating Doing Better

Thank You,
Maya Angelou

What do we mean when we say, "If we/they knew better, we/they would do better?"

Part of accepting this notion means accepting people in their innocent nature, understanding in a very real way that in their confusion, while living in this often crazy world, mistakes are made, and if they knew a better way, if they knew it in their hearts, they would have absolutely, without question, done better. Of course, this isn't a blank check for anyone to do anything they want without repercussions and consequences, but it is a way for us to see past the fearful cloud created by the mindless actions of people who aren't in touch with their authentic nature.

"Knowing better" is a tricky concept with multiple understandings which depend on where the "knowing better" is seated and functioning through. There needs to be a discernment between the intellectual rationalizing of the mind and the compassionate knowing of the heart. For example: We get that we shouldn't talk down to a loved one, but until we know it in our hearts, bring compassion and understanding to it from within ourselves, we don't really own it, it does not change our state of wellbeing, and we make the same mistakes over and over again. Authentic change requires full body contact; it requires a complete immersion in our truth. Until we know from the depths of our hearts, until we own it with every cell of our bodies, we are doomed to be seduced by and follow old, familiar patterns.

What cajoles us into mindless thoughts and actions that could only come from outside influence and misunderstanding of our truth? Is the fact that we often have old patterned mindless thinking guiding us a factor? And when we create suffering for ourselves and others could it be that we have not yet become clear in the truth of who we are, that we have not yet remembered the whisper of our own heart? The quality of our connection to the essence of our hearts impacts the world. This is a reality we must hold as precious and vitally important to all.

When you know better, when you really know it in your heart, you naturally do better. And if we're not doing better, it's because we haven't fully embraced the lesson placed in front of our heart. To do that, we have to see ourselves in psychological innocence, in a state of having forgiven ourselves for imperfect thinking and action, knowing that in all situations (and yes, this is redundant), if we had known a better way in our hearts, we would have absolutely done better.

We are not our mistakes. But our mistakes can guide us toward something more than what we have become. Our mistakes do not define who we are. We are defined far more by our desire to heal the pain we have caused for ourselves and others. We are defined by our recognition of the privilege to exist in this journey and our desire to understand the truth behind our existence. This is our journey, no one else's, and it is our strength, dedication, and action, all connected through thought, that helps us reconnect to that which provided us with the privilege of our life.

Knowing better
naturally cultivates
doing better.

"When we know better,
we do better."

-Maya Angelou

Sometimes we just have to get out of our heads about what life has presented to us and settle into our hearts about it. It's here that we find the secret of what it is to know something better so we can make the choice to live in some better way. Without the art of connecting to our heart, this "better" would be impossible.

The Hug

My grandfather was a lover. But he was born in 1911 and he came from a time when men only did manly kind of stuff. Being a "lover" wasn't exactly the craze in the early 1900s.

So let me start again.

My grandfather was a big, strong mountain of a man, Jack Buehler. He would trap, hunt, skin wild game, and sell the pelts and hides with one hand while rebuilding a Model T Ford with the other, all in an effort to make enough money to feed his family. This was all while school-aged. He didn't graduate high school because his father forced him to drop out in the ninth grade, reasoning that his son should be working for a living, making himself useful! Great Grandpa wanted Jack to be a man!

Enter, seventy years later, a skinny, long-haired hippy with goofy glasses, periodic bathing practices, questionable self-worth, pimples, and no hunting skills to boot. Not much to offer from a manly man perspective, but I did have an obsession for the books of Felice Leonardo "Leo" Buscaglia, PhD, also known as "Dr. Love." He talked on the power and presence of love in everyone, and how we should all be taking the opportunity to hug one another whenever we get a chance because after all, it may be our last chance (at least that's what I heard—the late seventies were a blast).

So I took advantage of Leo's wisdom and on one of my visits to the family lake house, Gramps got a big Dr. Love hug from his very questionable grandson. Not so surprisingly, for a moment, he froze, and then I thought he might try to wiggle to the ground, like a child on a playground, going limp because they didn't want to leave. He was obviously very embarrassed. I could palpably feel his conflict, holding back the urge to react more strongly, but un-mistakenly pushed me back, and with very wide eyes and a beautiful smile said, "Well, you made it. I have some beer in the refrigerator. Let's go sit on the dock." We both knew what happened, and we both gave it the space it needed so it could just be. Hugging men just wasn't something he was comfortable with. In my childhood, hugging was absolutely okay, but as a young man, we seem to have entered the hall of hugga-phobia!

Given Grampy's reaction and apparent repression of my attempts to love better, I was taken aback the next time I saw him. I believe it was later that day when he walked up to me and gave me a big beautiful grandfather-like hug, saying, "I guess it's okay for a grandfather to hug his grandson." It was a precious and beautiful moment burned into my heart, and it taught me a vital life lesson about embracing the art of "better," what it is to question where you are, what you think you know, and from there, what it is to know and to do better. This was from the heart—this is my brilliant example of someone who was willing to start again and choose love instead of fear.

When I remembered this story, which was lost in my mind for a few decades, and started writing about it, it brought me to tears. It's inspiring and touching to me when somebody can transition past their fear and then take the initiative to bring more love into the world. I think we're always touched in our hearts when a potentially painful situation becomes a loving one. Perhaps because we know human nature so well, we know that suffering can become our go-to emotion, the default way we approach things, and when we can avoid that door, it's time to celebrate joyfully!

At the end of every day, you have some questions to answer: How well did you love today, and how can you know and do better tomorrow?

*Cultivating
Doing Better*

---

*"The art of being wise
is the art of knowing what to overlook."*

-William James

In our innocence, we are all doing the best
that we can with the thoughts that we know
to give our attention to.

As we come to know a better way to think,
we also understand a better way to be.

Your problems are less about the world around you
and more about how you approach
the world around you.

The way we experience life
only changes when we change
how we choose to see it.

Life can always be lived better.
We can always strive to live a little more from the heart,
with less anxiety and a greater connection
to our spirit-driven spark of love.

This is the spark that defines us, that flows in
and through us; it's our true nature, it's our soul.

A part of connecting to our truth and seeing ourselves
with clarity is knowing that we always have the free
will choice to see our lives differently.

This puts the power of self-determined thought and
action in our own hands and allows us the freedom to
create whatever tone we choose for our lives.

So choose a tone, and choose with heart.

Authentic Strength

"One's philosophy is not best expressed in words;
it is expressed in the choices one makes.
In the long run, we shape our lives and we shape our-
selves. The process never ends until we die.
And the choices we make are ultimately
our own responsibility."

–Eleanor Roosevelt

No one creates emotional barriers for us
unless we agree to them.

Prepare to be disagreeable!

There's a point in our lives where we learn to "observe self," to watch ourselves with a clear awareness, to see our thinking and how our thoughts fold into our actions. Over time, we can learn to do this with great clarity, and we see, know, and understand ourselves in a better way.

Being aware of our mindful thoughts becomes apparent to us because our actions are the representations of the thinking that preceded them. Our actions reflect our mindful or mindless state of wellbeing in that moment. And in our more mindful times, the actions that manifest are based from a place that is good, and right, and compassionate. Without an over-inflated ego, we are proud of how we approach our life when we come from this more aware and responsible place.

That is mindfulness—when, in the present moment, whatever may be happening, we are in a place where we're minding, in full presentation, the life that we interact and co-create with.

The opposite, mindlessness, is carelessly reacting to our environment, and subsequently having less integrity, less awareness of our truth, and less clarity of our identity, which in turn, reflects an approach to life that is less "you."

Mindfully—more truth, more fully yourself.
Mindlessly—more fear, less of you, less yourself.

Never, ever live your life in the shadow
of another person's opinion about you.

This is the walk of life,
being alive in our deep presence in this place.

No one else can do the journey for you;
it's yours to take, alone.

Your journey, your lessons, painful and pleasurable,
your path is for you to walk, no one else—no friend,
spouse, preacher, or guru can do this for you,
and would you really want them to anyway?

Life is way too short and precious to spend it
chasing around other people's requirements
about how they want you to be.

Authentic
Strength

Everything we do is enhanced
when done with love
and compassion.

A Spiritual Warrior
(Honoring our Authentic Strength)

I'm a chiropractor by trade, and as one might guess, I tend to make a concerted effort to connect with all aspects of my patients in order to gain a more comprehensive view of how they're doing and what blockages and interferences need to be worked with. I start out most of my adjustments with the patient sitting on the table while I stand behind them and feel the tone of their muscles, looking for trigger points (the painful, hard, nodular knots that create so much body pain), checking for emotional stress points, and feeling the alignment of their spine. This gives me a minute to tune into them physically, emotionally, and often on a deeper spiritual level as well. Often, I get a sense of what's happening with a patient just from touch. Occasionally, it's more than that. This is about one of those moments.

One time a mental picture came to me while working on a patient. I was quite aware that he had some family struggles going on and my little vision directly related to that. As I began working out his tense, muscular trigger and stress points, this rather curious and un-expected picture entered my mind. It was of a Native American man standing tall and proud in the middle of a prairie, both feet planted strong and firmly on the ground, he was standing with a sense of authority. With one sweeping, precise movement, a physical act filled with intention and personal strength, he used both hands to grasp a long, modestly decorated spear and drove it into the ground directly in front of where he stood. In doing so, with obvious great intention and love, he was creating a safe space for his family. This spiritual warrior became the center of a circle where his family had permission to freely, safely, and with abandon to their truth, dance around him. They knew that he was there as support. He stood strong in this center, and if they needed him, they could count on his presence, he would be there. The warrior made his stand and created a space for himself and those he loved. He did his best to place himself into the position of patriarch, willfully taking on the role to advise, protect, and be on this journey with all who he touches.

We're all asked to do the same—to place ourselves in a space that allows those we love, as well as all parts of ourselves, to safely dance in the world with a deep abandon to our truth. We can only do our best with this given whatever our particular situation is in the moment, but we can always do our best. Our job is to keep the intention strong and bring a strength of love to ourselves and to all those we care for, no matter what the circumstance.

Authentic Strength

This intention, integrity, and personal volition towards love and truth is the natural product of knowing and honoring our authentic strength.

Change can seem precarious to the human psyche,
but thank God for it, because without it,
we would all die of boredom!

Being responsible for your own thinking, and thus your
actions is big, and worth paying attention to...
Why would you allow your thinking
to create anything but peace?

Peaceful thinking can often be mistaken
for passive thinking.
However, it is often the opposite.
Peaceful thought may indeed spur us toward
taking action in the name of love, justice,
or personal integrity.
Passivity is more a result of being scared
to move forward, regardless of the cause.

We are the only ones who can give ourselves
permission to open to a different,
gentler way of living.

Isn't that wonderful?

"Deep within man dwells those slumbering powers.
Powers that would astonish him,
that he never dreamed of possessing.
Forces that would revolutionize his life
if aroused and put into action."

-Orson Scott Marden

Feelings will always be a part of us,
but they do not have to define whether or not
we are able to step toward peace.
We do not have to give them dominion over
our free will choice to be who we are.

Try to keep in mind that you choose
the lens you look through as you walk forward
within this world.

This is a nice little mantra to say when the world
around us feels irrational and out of control.
It gives us permission to see it and not be it:
"Refuse to participate with crazy."

There is much freedom in understanding
that you are responsible for yourself.

Inspirational
Espresso

Be willing to be free.

- Be willing to stand strong in the midst of pain knowing that, in truth, you are indeed strong and the pain is at most temporary and often self-imposed.

- Be willing to escape from all prisons of the mind.

- Be willing to make peace with your expectation of what life should bring you. And remember, holding tight to your expectations is practice for disappointment.

- Be willing to let go enough to be in the moment of your next breath.

261

Be the type of person you wish

to surround yourself with!

Create for others the environment

that you want for yourself.

Neutralizing Judgment

*"It's not who you are that holds you back,
it's who you think you're not."*

-Unknown

*Letting go of our preconceptions and expectations,
we naturally allow better and often unexpected things
to come forward.*

There can be only one!

When we jump to judgment and fearfully interpret
the intentions of others as bad, we are unable to
connect with any kind of truth or understanding of
the issues that we need to address. We're unable to

see others or ourselves with any level of compassion, and healthy justice is usually nowhere to be found. We become hardened in our assumptions, seeing only the distorted ideas we hold and believing them to be true.

If we want truth and understanding and justice, we must temper it with compassion and kindness. We can only serve one essence, and fear just doesn't flow with understanding and love. There is no justice in fear.

We express judgment when we have fear regarding any situation. We have fear because we don't yet know how to understand and fully respond with the heart. And in the absence of our fearful judgment, we can find hope and all the good that comes through it.

Inspirational
Espresso

Does the chattering in your head that says, "You don't belong," have more to do with not belonging to yourself? Is it more about not accepting yourself and forever striving to be more, despite how wonderful you already are now?

This way of thinking begs the question: How hard do you judge others? Because that's the paradigm you will use to judge yourself with. How acceptable to you are the people in your world?

Give others what you want for yourself—open-hearted belonging.

" *H* ate is never conquered by hate.

Hate is only conquered by love."

-The Buddha

Simply put:
We get drawn into our judgment, pain, and fear
when we haven't figured out how to look
at something lovingly yet.

Neutralizing
Judgment

" *D* arkness cannot drive out darkness;

only light can do that.

Hate cannot drive out hate; only love can do that."

-Martin Luther King, Jr.

Other people can be so annoying to us—we can
barely stand looking at our faults in others!
They should be much better than that!

There are many times that it would suit us well
to recognize, accept, and celebrate that which
looks so different from our expectations
and how we think things "should" be.

How do we step past that person, place, or thing
that we think keeps us from living life?
How do we neutralize our judgment
and fear about them?
How do we choose to not think and
act the way of the victim?

The answer is inherent in the question, because it
involves choices made from and through the heart.
Our job is to remember how to do that.

Happiness, forgiveness, love—they all need
to be chosen from within.

It's not so much that we have to wait on them,
because they've already chosen us, and they're just
waiting for us to do the same.

"We create stress for ourselves because
you feel like you have to do it.
I don't feel that anymore."

-Oprah Winfrey

267

Judgment

Anything that makes us fearfully judgmental
toward anyone, including ourselves,
should be automatically understood as a
distortion of our mind,
a leaning into our fear.

"Argue for your limitations and sure enough,
they are yours."
-Richard Bach

We become imprisoned by the judgments we choose
to hold against others and against ourselves.
This is a most unloving place for us to live,
and its reward is our misery.

Concluding Sentiment

The riches of spirit belong to you;
no one can lay claim for you.

Your gift is the supreme privilege and
honor of being chosen—to be you.

Now, walk…walk in your truth,
Wherever you can find it,
Listen for it any way you can,
Grasp it, entangle yourself
however you are able.

Your destiny patiently awaits.
Accept the gift, knowing its presence
already exists within.

"*And you?*
When will you begin that
long journey into yourself?"
–Rumi